ENGT 170
Lab Manual

Projects and Handouts for Engineering Technology 170 at Rio Hondo Community College Whittier, CA

By: David Martin

Table of Contents

Introduction

Engineering Technology 170 Students:

The following is the Lab Manual for the ENGT 170 – MicroStation for Basic CADD Applications class. There are a number of projects to be completed during the course of the semester. Use the attached sheets to see what the projects look like.

The projects have been designed to give the student training in the use of the basic tools within the MicroStation software. Drafting practice will also be graded and it is recommended that current mechanical and architectural drafting practice be reviewed.

The class is divided into two parts. First, the entire class will complete the initial projects consisting one-view and two-view mechanical projects. Once these have been completed, the student will then complete the final project. This will consist of either a small mechanical assembly or a two room architectural project. Both of these projects are shown in the lab manual.

Students work at different rates and learn in different ways. If you find yourself finishing projects faster than other students, it is encouraged to work ahead. Please realize however, that this can sometimes be frustrating because a particular project may not have been covered in lecture prior to the student attempting it.

At the conclusion of the class you will assemble and submit a portfolio of your work. See the following pages for instructions.

Guidelines for successful completion of the projects:

1. Complete all projects using the appropriate title block/border.
2. Refer to the setup pages for the proper setup of each project.
3. Have your drawing checked by the instructor prior to printing. Major mistakes are usually found but a perfect score is not guaranteed.
4. When the drawing has been plotted turn in at the front desk.
5. If you have any questions about the projects please ask. Not all information is covered during lecture.

Before Beginning to Draw

Each project has a setup page that you aid you in drawing the project. The units that are used are either in millimeters, inches or architectural units. Before beginning the project, be sure to set up the file with the appropriate working units and levels. This will be covered during the first meeting. As the class progresses, the setup for new projects will change.

A good strategy is to develop a set of templates that have the various settings for each project already set up as part of the file. If a template does not exist, create one from a completed drawing.

Turning in Completed Projects

Projects will be graded at various times throughout the semester. Even though there are due dates assigned, late work will be accepted with a loss of 10% per week. Drawings must be plotted to receive credit and will be red-lined to show errors. In order to plot, the student must register for the open lab time class NVOC 018. This will give the student a $5.00 credit towards print costs. Once the initial $5.00 has been used the student must purchase a lab print card at the cashier's window.

You are allowed to turn in drawings once after they have been checked if they receive a grade of 80% or less. The initial grade and the new grade will be averaged. Re-submitting drawings is voluntary and should be done in a timely manner. The current syllabus will have due date information or will be announced in class.

Video Tutorials

There are on-line video tutorials available for student use at:

https://sites.google.com/site/davemartin131

ENGT 170 students will be given instructions on how to access this site and the tutorial files on the first day of class. Permission for others to access these files will be given as part of book purchase. The instructor may be contacted by email at **dave.martin131@gmail.com**. Please feel free to contact Dave Martin if you have any questions.

Title Blocks and Border Files

Title Blocks and Borders will be provided to the student. Most files are available on the Y: Drive and should be copied to your folder on the X: Drive. Some files will also be available on the class webpage.

Tests, Quizzes and Exams

There will be regular performance tests during the semester. You will be given a one week notice for each test. These tests will cover commands and techniques that were used up until that point in the class. Usually tests are less complicated than the projects but the student is responsible for setting up the drawing and completing the object without any assistance from other students or the instructor.

At the end of the course there will be a final exam. The exam will cover all topics from the beginning to the end of the class. There will also be a performance test that will evaluate the drawing ability of the student.

Working at Home

MicroStation has a policy of providing free software licenses for students. The software will be provided on the Y: for down to a student-supplied flash drive. The file size for the installation files is approximately 830MB. This way it will be possible to complete some of the class work at home. However, students are required to attend every class meeting and will be graded on their attendance. It is permissible for a student to complete some of the drawings at home but this is not a substitute for attending class.

File Management

One of the biggest problems during a computer-based skills class is the management of the various files created during the class. Since the lab that you will be working in is networked, you will be given space on the server (X: Drive) to store your drawing files. Do not use this space as the sole area to save your files. It is recommended that the student purchase a flash or USB drive to backup the work completed during the class.

File Management (continued)

Recommendations:
- Back-up drawings in one direction. Only copy files from the X: Drive to the flash drive.
- If you have worked on a drawing at home, copy only those files onto the X: drive. Be extremely careful not to overwrite a newer version of a file with an older version.
- Use folders to organize your work. A recommended method to do this will be covered during the first meeting.

Ending the Class

At the end of the class, time will be made available for the student to assemble a portfolio. Since the class meets once a week, the first three hours of the last class meeting will be used for this purpose. Prior to the final exam the student will turn in this portfolio for grading. All digital versions of the drawings will also be turned in to the instructor. This way, if a drawing is missing from the portfolio it may still be evaluated.

MicroStation Graphics User Interface

Shown below is the interface for the MicroStation design program. The first project is shown in the drawing area.

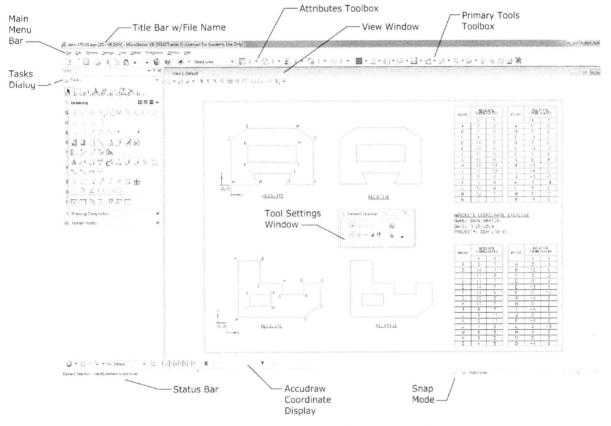

MicroStation V8i Select Series 3 Interface

Working Units Setup

Use this guide to setup drawing files with the correct working units. This must be done prior to beginning the drawing and will affect the size of elements if it is changed after the drawing has been started. Go to Settings, Design File to open the Design File Settings dialog box.

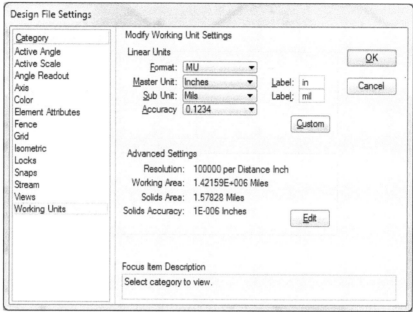

Working Units Setting

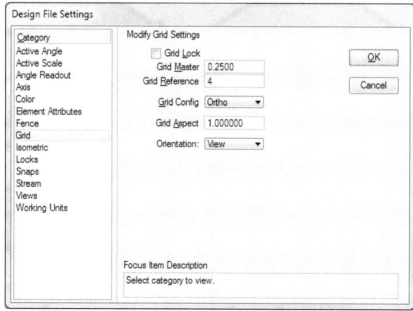

Grid Setting

Use the following setup for mechanical drawings in imperial measurement (inches)

Format: **MU**	Resolution: **100000 per Distance Inch**
Master Unit: **Inches**	Grid Master: **0.2500**
Sub Unit: **Mils**	Grid Reference: **4**
Accuracy: **0.1234**	

Use the following setup for mechanical drawings in metric measurement (millimeters)

Format: **MU**	Resolution: **100000 per Distance Inch**
Master Unit: **Millimeters**	Grid Master: **6.3500**
Sub Unit: **Micrometers**	Grid Reference: **4**
Accuracy: **0.1234**	

Use the following setup for architectural drawings in feet and inches

Format: **MU:SU**	Resolution: **10000 per Distance Meter**
Master Unit: **Feet (')**	Grid Master: **1:0**
Sub Unit: **Inches (")**	Grid Reference: **4**
Accuracy: **1/64**	

Note: The resolution for this setup is not changed. The default setting in the Seed2d.dgn file is 10000 per Meter.

Mechanical Drawing Level Setup

Go to the Primary Tools tool palette to setup the Levels for a drawing. Click on the Level Manager tool to open the Level manager Dialog box.

Primary Tools Tool Palette

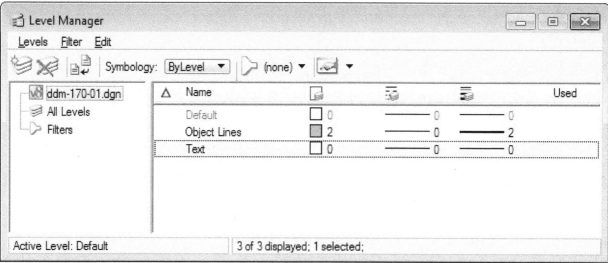

Level Manager Dialog Box

Use the following level setup for both imperial and metric drawings:

Level Name	Color	Style	Weight
Object Lines	Green (2)	0	2
Hidden Lines	White (0)	(Hidden)	0
Center Lines	White (0)	(Center) or (Center-Short)	0
Dimensions	White (0)	0	0
Text	White (0)	0	0
Hatching	Red (3)	0	0
Border Lines*	Yellow (4)	0	2
Points*	Magenta (5)	0	6
Tags*	White (0)	0	0

*Used for A-Size and B-Size Border Files.

Architectural Drawing Level Setup

Use the following level setup for architectural drawings. Some levels may not be used on certain drawings:

Level Name	Color	Style	Weight
Border Lines	Yellow (4)	0	2
Casework	Magenta (5)	0	0
Concrete	Yellow (4)	0	2
Default	White (0)	0	0
Dimensions	White (0)	0	0
Dimension - Thick	Red (3)	0	2
Doors	Green (2)	0	0
Fixtures	Red (3)	0	0
Footer	White (0)	(Hidden)	2
Framing	Green (2)	0	2
Hidden	White (0)	(Hidden)	0
Inside Edges	White (0)	0	0
Landscape	Dark Green (66)	0	0
Patterning	Light Gray (9)	0	0
Patterning Boundary	Light Gray (9)	0	0
Points	Green (2)	0	6
Property Line	White (0)	(Phantom)	3
Rebar	Red (3)	0	2
Roof Edge	Red (3)	0	2
Tags	White (0)	0	0
Text	White (0)	0	0
Thin	Magenta (5)	0	0
Utility Lines	White (0)	Varies	0
Walls	Yellow (4)	0	2
Windows	Cyan (7)	0	0

Note: Use this to begin the process of level setup. You wish to add additional levels besides the ones shown above.

Drawing Setup for the Initial 2D Projects

This chart shows the various settings for the initial 12 mechanical projects.

Drawing Name	Drawing Scale	Print Scale	Dimension Text Size	Linestyle Scale Factor	Grid Dot Spacing
Project #1	None	Maximize	.500	N/A	N/A
Project #2	None	Maximize	.200	N/A	N/A
Project #3	1:1	1.000	.125	1.000	.2500
Project #4	1:1	1.000	.125	1.000	.2500
Project #5	1:1	1.000	.125	1.000	.2500
Project #6	1:2	2.000	.250	2.000	.500
Project #7	1:2	2.000	.250	2.000	.500
Project #8	1:1 (Metric)	25.400	3.175	1.000	6.350
Project #9	1:2 (Metric)	50.800	6.350	2.000	12.700
Project #10	10:1	.100	.0125	.100	.025
Project #11	1:1	1.000	.125	1.000	.250
Project #12	1:1 (Metric)	25.4	3.175	1.000	6.350

Project Volumes for Initial 3D Projects

1. Use these volumes as a guide when turning in the 3D version of your projects.
2. The tolerance is the amount that your volume can differ from the volume shown. The +/- means that the volume can be above or below the amount shown by the given value.
3. Use the **Measure Volume** tool in the **Measure** palette to measure the volume of your project.

Drawing Name	Volume	Units	Tolerance	
Project #1A (Part is 1" Thick.)	105.0000	Cubic Inches	+/- .000 (No Tolerance)	105.000
Project #1B (Part is 1" Thick.)	87.000	Cubic Inches	+/- .000 (No Tolerance)	87.000
Project #2 (Part is 1" Thick.)	26.7764	Cubic Inches	+/- .000 (No Tolerance)	26.7764
Project #3	4.9647	Cubic Inches	+/- .010	4.9747 4.9547
Project #4	2.1215	Cubic Inches	+/- .010	2.1315 2.1115
Project #5	9.5652	Cubic Inches	+/- .010	9.5752 9.5552
Project #6	9.7844	Cubic Inches	+/- .010	9.7944 9.7744
Project #7	1.2367	Cubic Inches	+/- .002	1.2387 1.2347
Project #8	29370.967	Cubic Millimeters	+/- 2.000	29372.967 29368.967
Project #9	117879.0256	Cubic Millimeters	+/- 2.000	117881.0256 117877.0256
Project #10	0.01323	Cubic Inches	+/- .0002	0.01343 0.01303
Project #11	0.6732	Cubic Inches	+/- .002	0.6752 0.6712
Project #12	88452.172	Cubic Millimeters	+/- 2.000	88454.172 88450.172

Initial Projects

Project #1

Name: Absolute Coordinate Exercise
File Name: Initials-170-01.dgn

Description: The project has been designed to give the student practice in the use of the data point key-in window. This window allows the student to key-in coordinates in either absolute or relative coordinates.

Tools:
- Place Line
- Place Text
- Edit Text
- Fit View

Starting the software

1. Find and click on the MicroStation Icon to start the software.

Microstation Icon

2. The splash screen will appear. Wait for the software to open and for the File Manager dialog box to open.

File Manager Dialog Box

3. Set up a folder structure for your drawing files. Start by creating a folder called "ENGT 170" on your flash drive or hard drive. Use the Create New Folder tool in the File Manager dialog.

New Folder Tool

4. Create a sub-folder under the ENGT 170 Files folder called "Initial Projects". Double click on the folder to open it.

    This will be where you will store the first 12 projects of the book.

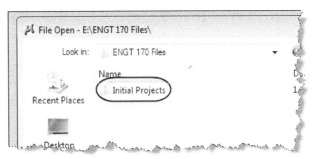

Initial Projects Folder

5. Click on the New File tool to create a file located at the top of the dialog box.

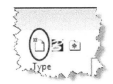

New File Command

6. Verify that the Seed File to be used is seed2d.dgn.

    This file contains the settings that are used for the initial setup of the file. Later we will use other methods to apply these settings to new files.

seed2d.dgn Seed File

7. The New Dialog box will open. Type in the file name in the File name field below.

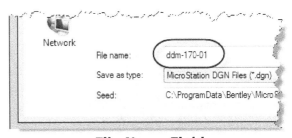

File Name Field

8. Click the Save button at the lower right corner of the dialog box.

    In the default setting of the software, you must name a file before opening it.

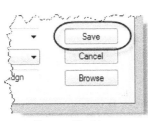

Save Button

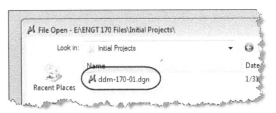

File Created

9. Open the file by double clicking on it or by pressing the Open button in the File Open Dialog box.

    This dialog box shows the files in a particular folder and a preview or thumbnail of the file when it was last saved. You can also setup User, Project, and Interface setting at the bottom right corner. You will not be using these in this book.

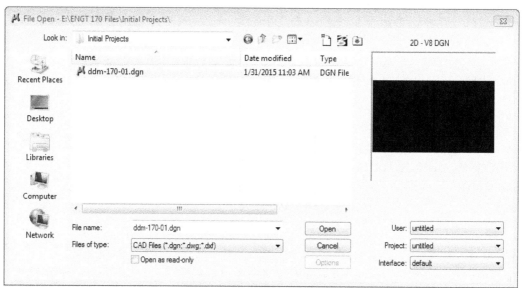

File Open Dialog Box

10. The Microstation Interface opens. By default the background is black with white gridlines and dots. Images in the book with use a white background for clarity.

    If you wish to change this setting, click on the Workspace menu at the top and select Preferences.

    The Preferences dialog box will open. Select View Options category from the list on the left and check the box next to "Black Background -> White".

    Click the OK button to close the box.

    Later, we will re-visit this box to make other changes to the Preferences.

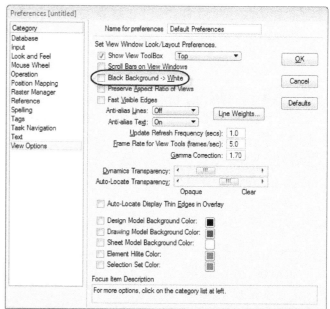

Preferences Dialog Box – View Options Category Change

11. Also turn on the Save Settings on Exit setting.

    This way, if you make changes to any off the drawing file settings they will be saved after exiting the file. This setting is in the Operation category.

    Note: Saving the drawing will not save the drawing settings.

**Preferences Dialog Box – Operations
Category Change**

12. If you are an AutoCAD user or would like to use the ESC (Escape) key to end the command, use the Input category in the Preferences dialog to turn on the feature.

**Preferences Dialog Box – Input
Category Change
Allow ESC key to stop current command**

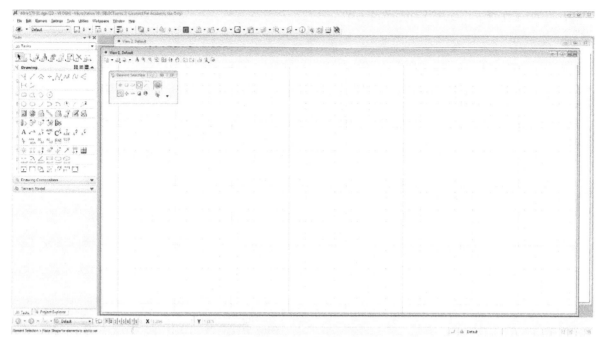

Default User Interface

13. Before beginning the drawing, you must set the working units for the file. See the working units setup page for values. Since this drawing is an Imperial (Inches) drawing, we will use the following settings for the Working Units.

14. Click on the Settings Menu, Design File.

15. The Design File Settings dialog box opens. Select the Working Units category.

16. Setup the workings units as shown. Click on the Edit button to change the Resolution.

   A warning box will appear. Click the OK button to continue.

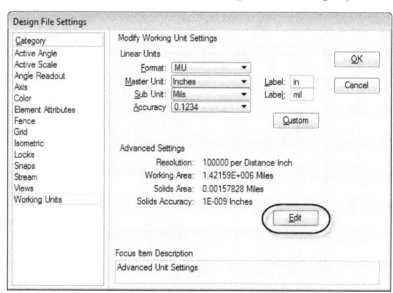

Design File Settings Dialog

17. Set the Advanced Unit Setting as shown.

    Do not change the Working Areas field.

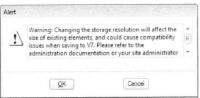

**Alert Box
(Working Units Change)**

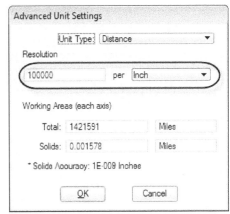

Advanced Unit Settings Dialog

Note: Working units are typically setup at the beginning of the project and are not changed. If the settings are changed then the project sizes and locations could also change. If you are working on a project with other designers, the working units will typically be specified by the Project Manager.

18. Close the Design File Settings dialog to change the Working Units. Re-open the dialog to change the Grid setting.

19. Set the Grids as shown.

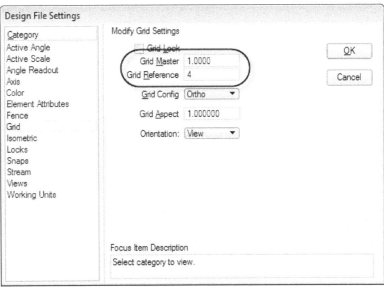

Grid Dot Settings

20. If you cannot see the Grids on the screen, use the wheel on your mouse to zoom in and out. You will also be able to see the grids after beginning the drawing and fitting the view.

21. Click on the Level Manager tool at the top of the screen. In the Create two layers. Name one layer **Object Lines** and the other **Text**.

Level Manager Tool

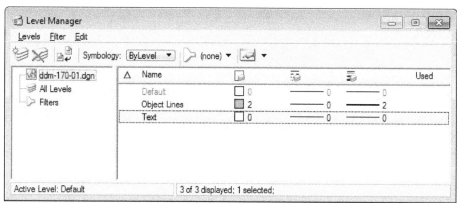

Level Manager Dialog Box

22. Before adding your first line, set the level to Object Lines. Do this by choosing the Object Line level at the top left of the screen.

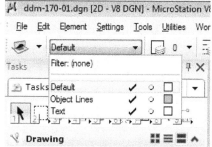

Selecting the Level

23. Open the data point key-in window. To do this, select the Accudraw Coordinate window and press the **M** key. Use this window to enter coordinates for the various points on the shapes.

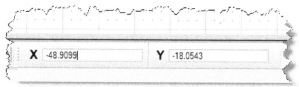

Accudraw Coordinate Window

24. The Data Point Keyin window will open. Use the Absolute (xy=) setting to add the coordinates for the line endpoints.

Data Point Keyin Window

25. Start with the first shape in the upper left corner of the example using the Absolute(xy=) option. Use the Line Tool in the Drawing palette.

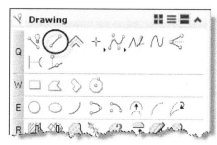

Line Tool

26. After adding the first line, fit the object in the view using the Fit View tool. This tool is located at the tool of the drawing view window.

Fit View Tool

Continue to use this tool to fit the objects as they are added to the drawing.

Note: You can also zoom in and out by using the wheel on your mouse. To pan the view, hold the wheel down and move the mouse.

27. Use the chart in the Project #1 drawing to key-in the coordinates.

28. Continue with the second version of the same shape using the Delta(dl=) option.

POINT	ABSOLUTE COORDINATES		POINT	RELATIVE COORDINATES	
	X	Y		X	Y
A	0	0	A	0	0
B	5	0	B	5	0
C	4	2	C	−1	2
D	11	2	D	7	0
E	10	0	E	−1	−2
F	15	0	F	5	0
G	15	8	G	0	8
H	12	10	H	−3	2
I	3	10	I	−9	0
J	0	8	J	−3	−2
K	3	4	K	3	−4
L	12	4	L	9	0
M	12	7	M	0	3
N	3	7	N	−9	0

Project #1 Chart Absolute Coordinate Chart

Relative Coordinate Chart

29. Complete the two versions of the second shape using the appropriate method.

Setting Up the Outside Border and Text Boxes

1. Draw the outside border. Use 65.8 for the width and 44.4 for the height. Use the Absolute Coordinate method and the Place Block tool.

Place Block Tool

2. Setup the frame for the first text box. The total width of the box is **9.0** and each column is **3.0**. The height of each row is **1.0**. Drawing the box using the Place Line tool.

3. After placing the two vertical lines and the top line, use to Move Parallel tool to copy the lines down from the top.

    Access the tool by clicking and holding on the third tool in the Main palette. You may also open the Manipulate toolbox by selecting "Open 'Manipulate' as toolbox".

Manipulate Toolbox

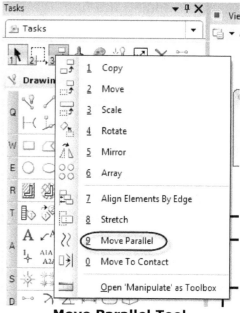

Move Parallel Tool

4. Use 2.000 for the first line and then 1.000 for the remaining lines.

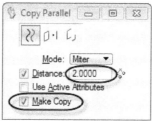

Move/Copy Parallel Settings

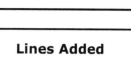

Lines Added

5. Add two vertical lines from the left or right side using the Copy Parallel command at a distance of 3.000.

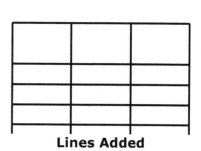

Lines Added

6. Use the Trim To Element tool to trim the lines.

    You may also to open the Modify toolbox to access the tools quickly.

Modify Toolbox

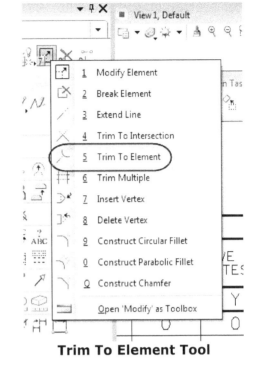

Trim To Element Tool

7. When trimming, click the portion of the element that you will be trimming first then click the element that you are trimming to second.

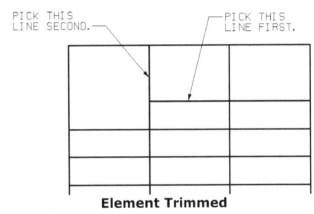

Element Trimmed

8. Continue trimming until the text box appears as in the project example.

9. Next you will need to create two separate lines from the second vertical line. Use the Break Element tool to create two lines and the trim to to connect them to the horizontal line.

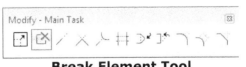
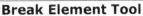

Break Element Tool

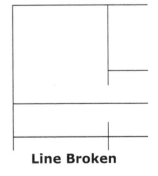

Line Broken

10. After reattaching the two line segments, select the lines that appear thinner in the example.

    Click in the Level selector pulldown at the top left of the screen and change the level for the line to Text.

    They will appear thinner and white (or black) in color.

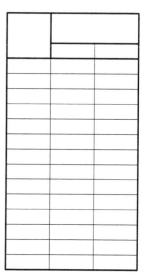

Completed Lines for Table

11. Setup the text for the first column. Use .5 for the text height and width. The line spacing is 1.0 and the line space style is set to Exact. Use Top, Center for the justification. The smaller text at the top is .375, justification is Center, Center.

Place Text Tool

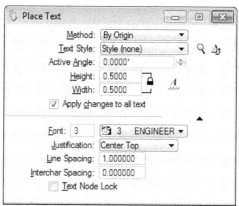

Place Text dialog with text settings applied.

12. Type the entire first column all at once and place the first row in the first cell of the table.

    When placing the text use the Snap function to lock the text at the intersection of the two lines.

Column of text for first column

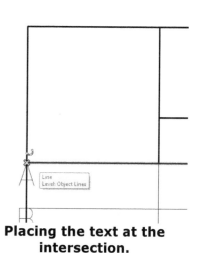

Placing the text at the intersection.

13. Use the Move tool to move the text into the correct location.

Move Tool

Moving the text to the correct location.

14. Use these steps to move the text using the Accudraw window.

    a. Select the text column.
    b. Click the Move tool.
    c. Click the start point for the move.
    d. Move the text down and to the right.
    e. Type 1.5, then the Tab key, then .25 (the value should be negative).
    f. Click to complete the moving of the text.

15. Complete the remaining text for the columns.

16. To place the text for the POINT and ABSOLUTE COORDINATES boxes use the settings as shown.

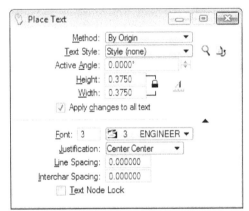

Text settings for the two upper boxes.

17. To aid in locating the text, draw two temporary diagonal lines and snap the text to the midpoint of the lines.

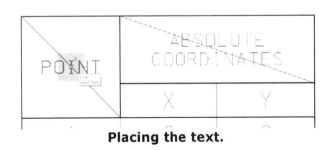

Placing the text.

18. Once the first table has been completed. Copy the table three times and edit the text. It is much easier to edit existing text than create new text.

    Use the Accudraw window and the Move tool to move and place the tables. The tables are 1.000 from the corners of the border and from each other.

19. Type the name of the project, your name, date, and the project # between the four text tables.

    You will need to create a separate text line for the underlined text since you cannot combine underlined and non-underlined text.

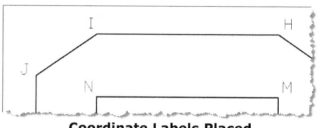

ABSOLUTE & RELATIVE COORD. EXER.
NAME: DAVE MARTIN
DATE: 5-17-2014
PROJECT#: DDM-170-01

Drawing Label Text

20. Place the text for coordinate labels at the corners of the top left and top right shapes. Use .5 for the text height.

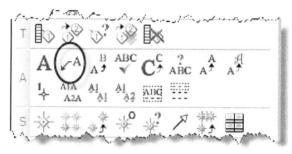

Coordinate Labels Placed

21. Place the origin symbols at the lower left corners the two left shapes. You will use the place note command to place the arrows.

Place Note tool

22. To set the size of the arrowhead you will need to open the Dimension Styles dialog box. Click on the Element Menu, Dimension Styles to do this.

23. Match the settings as shown.

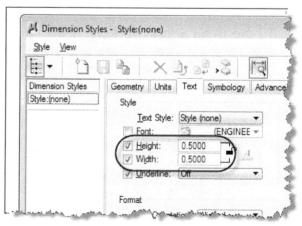

Text Settings in Dimension Styles Dialog

24. Add the text and arrows as shown.

    For the second origin symbol, the origin is offset 2.000 to the left and 1.000 down from the corner of the view.

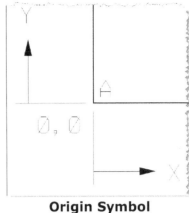

Origin Symbol

25. Save the file.

    Note: In the default setup of MicroStation, the file is saved automatically after a change has been made to the drawing. Although not required for these projects, this setting may be turned off in the Preferences dialog box under the Operation category.

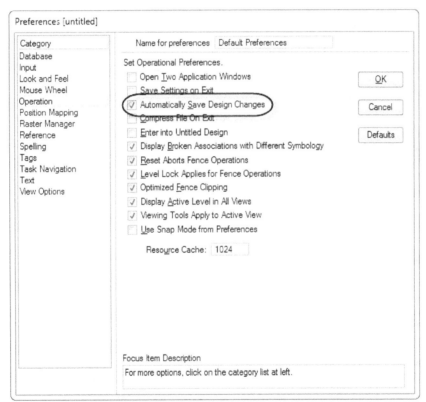

Automatically Save Changes checkbox

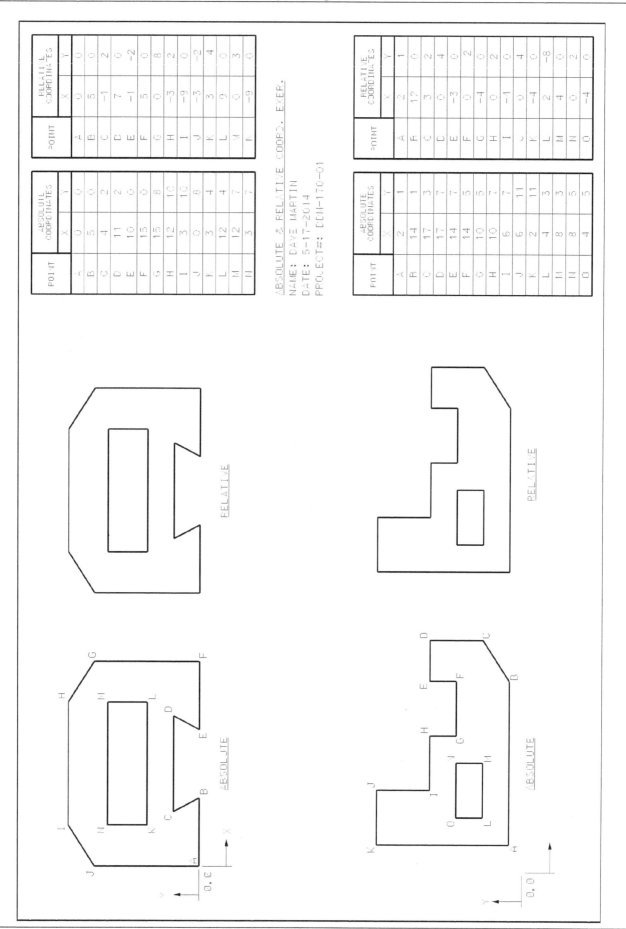

ABSOLUTE & RELATIVE COORD. EXER.
NAME: DAVE MARTIN
DATE: 5-17-2014
PROJECT#: DCM-170-01

Left shape — ABSOLUTE COORDINATES

POINT	X	Y
A	0	1
B	5	0
C	4	2
D	11	2
E	10	0
F	15	0
G	15	8
H	12	10
I	3	10
J	0	8
K	3	4
L	12	4
M	12	7
N	3	7

Left shape — RELATIVE COORDINATES

POINT	X	Y
A	0	0
B	5	0
C	-1	2
D	7	0
E	-1	-2
F	5	0
G	0	8
H	-3	2
I	-9	0
J	-3	-2
K	3	4
L	9	0
M	0	3
N	-9	0

Right shape — ABSOLUTE COORDINATES

POINT	X	Y
A	2	1
B	14	1
C	17	3
D	17	7
E	14	7
F	14	5
G	10	5
H	10	7
I	6	7
J	6	11
K	2	11
L	4	3
M	8	3
N	8	5
O	4	5

Right shape — RELATIVE COORDINATES

POINT	X	Y
A	2	1
B	12	0
C	3	2
D	0	4
E	-3	0
F	0	-2
G	-4	0
H	0	2
I	-1	0
J	0	4
K	-4	0
L	2	-8
M	4	0
N	0	2
O	-4	0

RELATIVE

ABSOLUTE

0.0

Project #2

Name: Relative Coordinate Exercise
File Name: Initials-170-02.dgn

Description: The project has been designed to give the student additional practice in the use of the data point key-in window.

Tools:
- Place Line
- Place Text
- Edit Text
- Fit View

Procedure:

1. Open Project #1 and save the drawing as Project #2.

   Note: If you are immediately starting the project just after completing Project #1, save the file before using the Save As… command to save as Project #2.

2. Keep the same level setup as Project #1.

3. Open the data point key-in window. Click on the accudraw coordinate window and press the M key. Use this window to enter coordinates for the various points on the shapes.

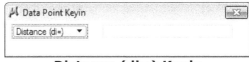
Distance (di=) Keyin

4. Click the first point with the mouse. Use the Data Point Keyin window for the remaining lines.

5. When keying in the points, use the Distance(di=) option. The first number is the length of the line, the second is the angle.

Key-in for first line.

6. To draw the line from M to A, use the endpoint snap function.

7. To check the angle to eight place decimal accuracy you will need to change the accuracy setting in the Design File Settings dialog box.

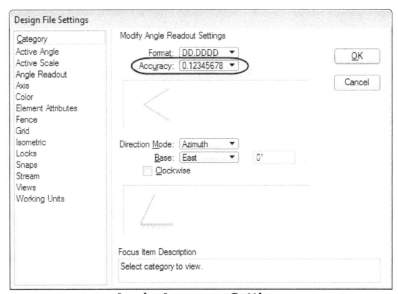
Angle Accuracy Settings

8. To check the distance to six place decimal accuracy you will need to change the accuracy setting in the Design File Settings dialog box.

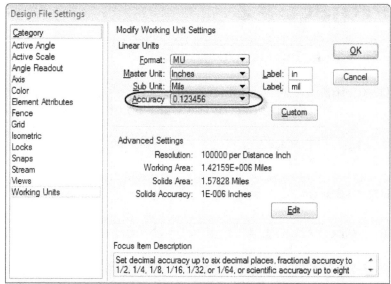

Distance Accuracy Settings

9. Verify that the line is the correct length and angle using the Information tool located at the top right of the screen. Click on the line and then the tool.

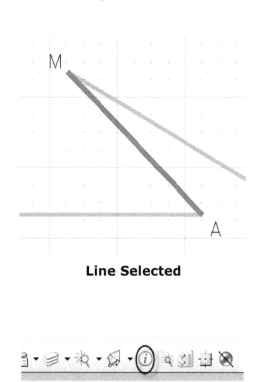

Line Selected

Information tool

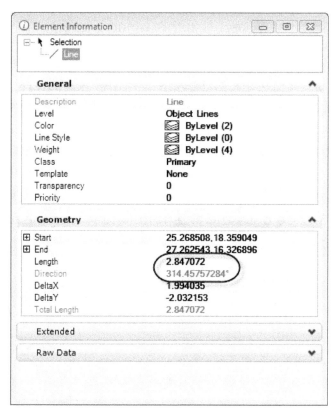

10. When completed with the object, draw the outside border. Use 15.7 for the width and 8.7 for the height.

11. Position the border in relation to the completed shape.

12. Type in the text for the title, name, date, and project name. Use .2 for the text height and width. Use Left Top for the justification and .75 for the line spacing.

    Note:
    As in Project #1 you will need to create separate text elements for the underlined text.

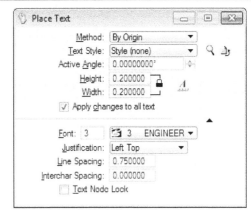

Text Settings for text.

13. Copy the text or type in the values for the point distances and angles and for the length and angle for point M to A.

14. Place the text at the corners of the top left and top right shapes. Use .2 for the text height.

15. Save the drawing.

RELATIVE COORDINATE EXERCISE

NAME: DAVE MARTIN
DATE: 5-17-2014
PROJECT#: DDM-170-02

A = START
B = 3.75", 180°
C = 2.38", 150°
D = 1.75", 45°
E = 2.19", 135°
F = 3.62", 15°
G = 1.50", 285°
H = 2.06", 15°
J = 1.12", 120°
K = 2.75", 330°
L = 3.62", 270°
M = 4.12", 150°

M TO A
LENGTH = 2.847072",
ANGLE IN XY PLANE =
314.45757284°

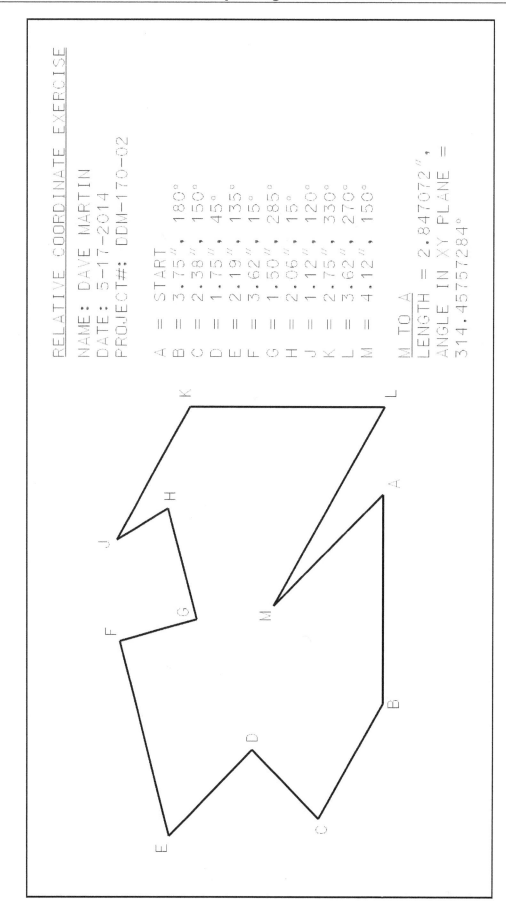

Project #3

Name: Conveyor Link
File Name: Initials-170-03.dgn

Description: The project will introduce the student the concept of referencing, dimensioning, and linestyles.

Tools:
- Place Line
- Place Circle
- Construct Circular Fillet
- Attach Reference

- Merge Into Master
- Dimension Linear
- Dimension Radial
- Dimension Diameter

- Edit Text
- Edit Tags
- Fit View
- Partial Delete

Procedure:

Setting Up the Drawing File

1. Open Project #2 and save the drawing as Project #3.

2. Refer to the level setup page for the levels to create and their properties. There will be additional levels added to this drawing. Refer to the diagram for their names and properties.

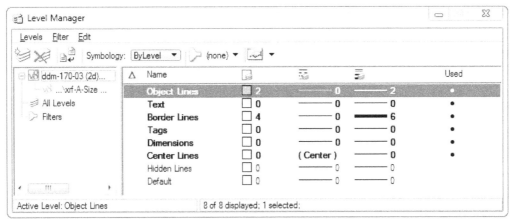

Level Setup for Project #3

3. Attach the **xrf-A-Size Border** and **xrf-Title Block Text (A-Size)** files as reference files.

   Note: The term "Referencing Files" means that you will be attaching a link from one file to another. The result of this is that the file that is linked may be updated and the changes will appear in the file that it is linked to. For Projects 3-12 you will be linking the Border and Title Block Text files onto the drawing. These files are located on the ENGT 170 page of the website.

4. Download and Copy the files **xrf-A-Size Border.dgn** and **xrf-Title Block Text (A-Size).dgn** from the ENGT 170 Documents page. You should copy all the files and save on your local drive. Create a folder called Title Blocks to contain the files.

5.   Click on the References tool at the top of the screen.

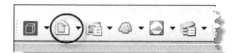

References Tool

6.   This will open the References Dialog box.

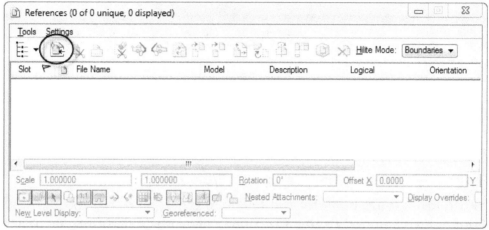

References Dialog Box (Attach Reference tool circled)

7.   Click on the Attach Reference Tool and select the two files mentioned in Step #4. Also check the Save Relative Path checkbox at the bottom. If you change computers and the drive letters change the file will still maintain the link.

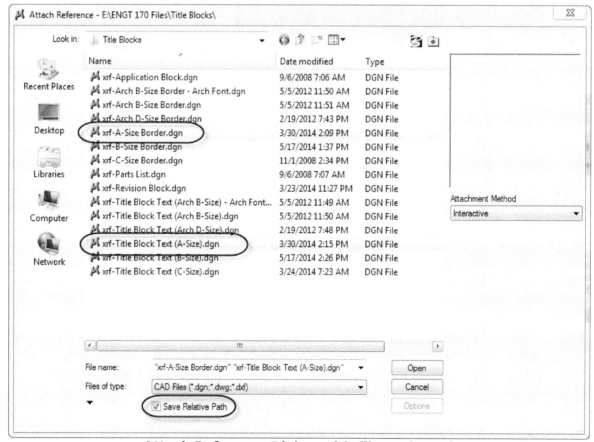

Attach Reference Dialog with files selected

8. The files will be attached to the drawing.

   As they are added the Reference Attachment Settings dialog box opens.

   Click the OK button to attach the file.

   This dialog box will be covered in more detail in later projects.

Reference Attachment Settings Dialog Box

9. Merge the text file into the drawing.

   Do this by right-clicking on the file in the list of linked files.

   Select the Merge Into Master choice. Note that it says at the bottom corner to Select View for Merge...

   Click in the view window to complete the process.

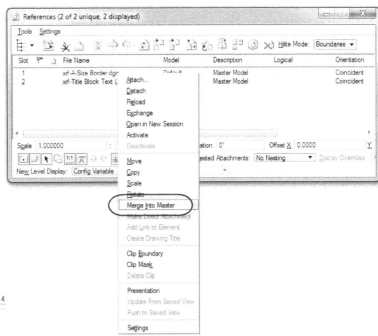

10. To edit the text in the title block, double-click on one of the text elements.

Use the Edit Tags dialog box to edit the text in the title block.

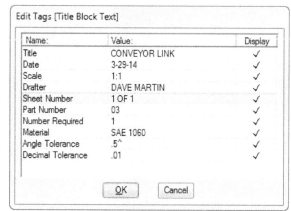

Edit Tags Dialog Box

Drawing the Object

1. Set the current level to Object Lines using the Attributes toolbox. Make sure that the Color, Linestyle, and Lineweight are set to By Level. This is indicated by the stack of white papers showing next to each setting.

Attributes Toolbox

2. Draw the two R.81 arcs as circles 6.00 apart. You may also draw one circle and copy it 6.00 to the right or left.

Use a temporary construction line to locate the second circle accurately.

Place Circle Tool

3. When setting up the circle, use the Tool Settings dialog box that appears after selecting the tool.

Check the Radius checkbox and enter .81 as the radius.

You may also change the entry type by clicking on the radius pulldown.

Place Circle Tool Settings Box

Two Circles with Temporary Construction Line

4. Add two lines at the top and bottom of the circles. Make sure to snap the lines using the Quadrant Snap Mode to the top and bottom of the circle.

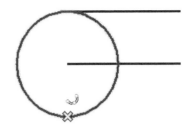

Line start point locked at bottom of circle

About Snaps

Snaps are used to lock new elements at various points on existing objects. You may turn on the snap mode button bar by clicking on the Snap Mode tool at the bottom of the screen. The Snap Mode Button Bar allows you to switch quickly between one snap mode and another.

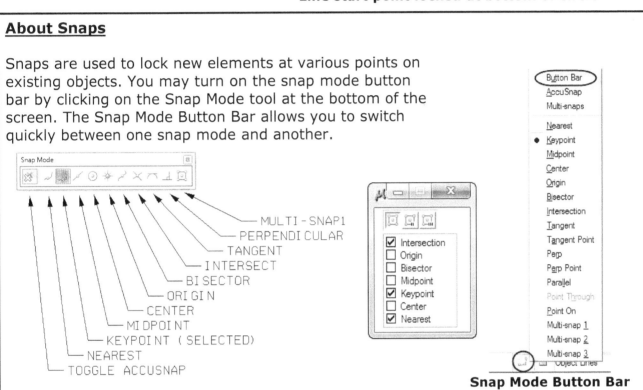

Snap Mode Button Bar and Multi-Snap Dialog

Snap Mode Button Bar Selection

- By clicking once on the desired snap mode, the mode will be active for one command. If you double click on the mode then it will remain active until you choose another mode.

- If you want to use multiple modes at once, use the Multi-snap tool at the end of the button bar. Open the dialog box by right-clicking and selecting Settings. You may setup three Multi-snap modes.

- By using the AccuSnap toggle, you can turn automatic snapping on or off.

- Drag the button bar to the bottom of the screen to dock it next to the Accudraw coordinate box.

5. Draw the two .56 diameter circles in the centers of the larger circles.

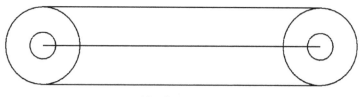

Circle Added

6. Draw a R3.88 arc concentric with the right circle.

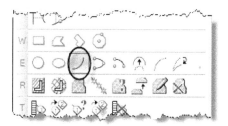

Arc Tool

Use these settings for the arc.

Arc Settings

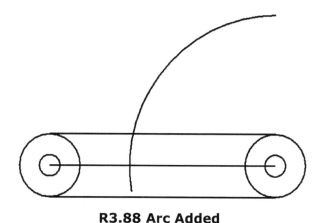

R3.88 Arc Added

7. Use the Move Parallel tool to create the other four lines that make up the edge of the object and the slot. Refer to the drawing example for sizes.

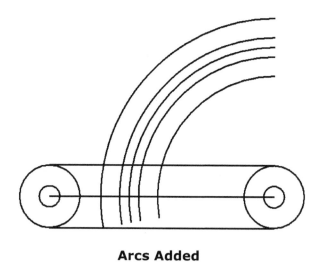

Arcs Added

8. Add two lines starting at the center of the right circle. Draw one line at 120 degrees and the other at 165 degrees.

9.   Add two R.25 arcs at the intersection of the angled lines and the R3.88 circle. Use the mouse to draw them long enough to intersect the edges of the other arcs.

Use the Snaps Button Bar to temporarily activate the Intersection Snap.

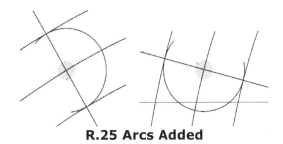

R.25 Arcs Added

10. Add the R.75 Arc at the top of the view.

Try snapping at the intersections when placing the arc endpoints.

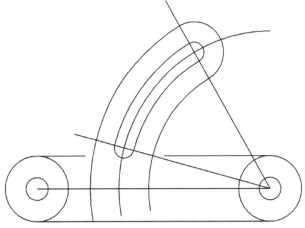

Adding the R.75 Arc

11. Trim the corners and tangencies using the Trim to Intersection tool.

Trim to Intersection Tool

12. Break the line connecting the tops of the two R.81 circles.

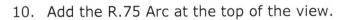

Line Broken and Intersections Trimmed

13. Fillet the two corners at R1.25 and R.75. The lines will trim and extend when creating the fillet arcs.

Construct Circular Fillet Tool

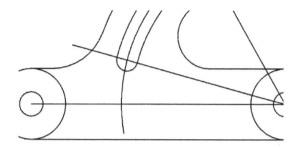

Fillets Created

14. Break the two R.81 arcs towards the inside.

Trim the arc and the horizontal lines at the top and bottom of the arcs.

Delete the construction lines.

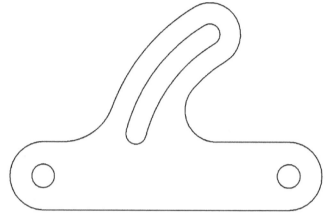

View Completed

Adding the Center Lines and Dimensioning the View

Before adding the center lines to the view, you will need to load a custom linestyle file created for this manual. You will use these lines styles for all the projects.

1. Download and copy the files from the ENGT 170 Documents webpage to your flash drive or hard drive. You should create a new subfolder on your drive called Linestyles.
   The two files are called: **Arch_linestyle.rsc** and **acadlsty.rsc**.

2. To load the linestyle file click on the Element Menu, Linestyles, Edit

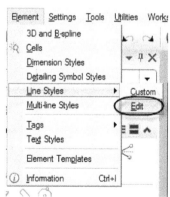

Element Menu Command

3. The Line Style Editor box opens. You will use this dialog box to load the linestyle file.

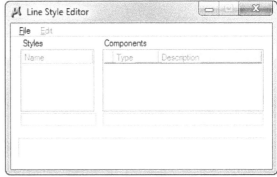

Line Style Editor box

4. In the dialog box, click on File, Import, MicroStation Resource File (RSC)... to load the file.

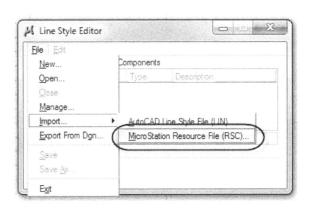

5. Select the **acadlsty.rsc** file to load.

    Note: The other file will be used for the architecture projects later in the manual.

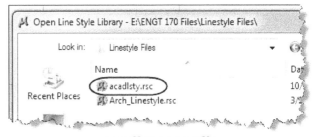

acadlsty.rsc File

6. The Select Linestyles to Import dialog box will open. Select all of the linestyles to load into your file. Click the Import button to complete the load.

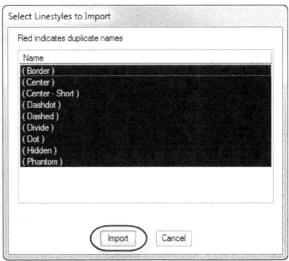

Select Linestyles to Import Dialog Box

7. Click on the Linestyle pulldown at the top of the screen.

    You will see the linestyle names that were loaded.

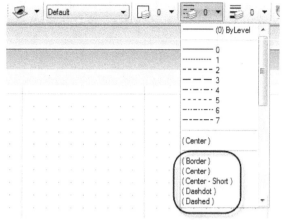

Linestyle Pulldown

8. Switch to the Center Lines level.

9. Draw the center lines as shown in the example.

    If you do not see the dashes appear, check the in Level Manager to confirm that the Center Lines level is using the (Center) linestyle.

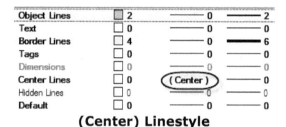

(Center) Linestyle

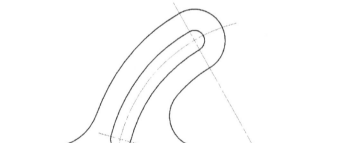

Center Lines Added

Setting Up the Dimension Style

Before you can dimension the drawing you will need to create a dimension style. Over the next few steps you will create a new dimension style and apply changes to match the example.

10. Open the Dimension Styles dialog box by clicking on the Element menu and selecting Dimension Styles.

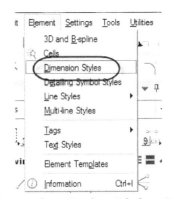

Dimension Styles Dialog Box

11. The Dimension Styles dialog box opens. Click on the Create Style tool and name it as shown.

Make the changes as shown in the circled areas. All other settings will remain the same. Press the Save Button to save the changes after leaving each tab. If a change or style has not been saved it will appear blue.

You will see the style update at the bottom of the dialog after each change.

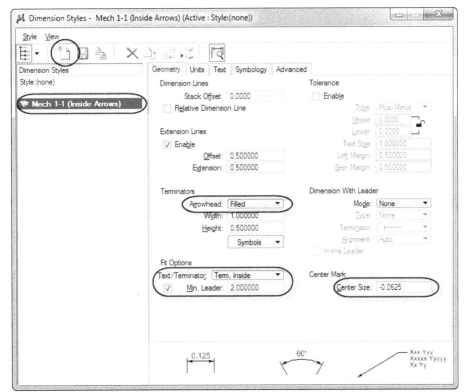

Dimension Style Dialog Box – Geometry Tab Changes

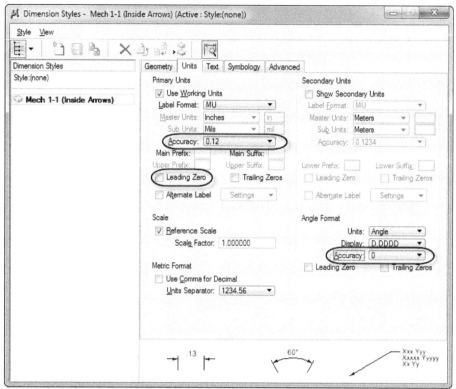

Dimension Style Dialog Box – Units Tab Changes

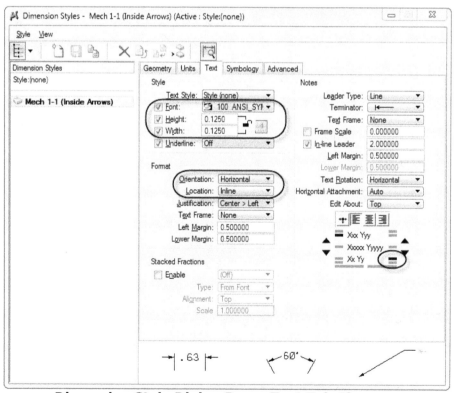

Dimension Style Dialog Box – Text Tab Changes

There will be no changes to the Symbology Tab. The reason for making any changes would be if you wanted to override the properties of the level settings for the Dimension level.

When making changes to the Advanced Tab, open the Tool Specific Property and set the prefix for Radius, Radius Extended, Diameter, and Diameter Extended to None.

The reason for this is because you will need to edit some of the dimensions to place the 2X in front of the dimension value.

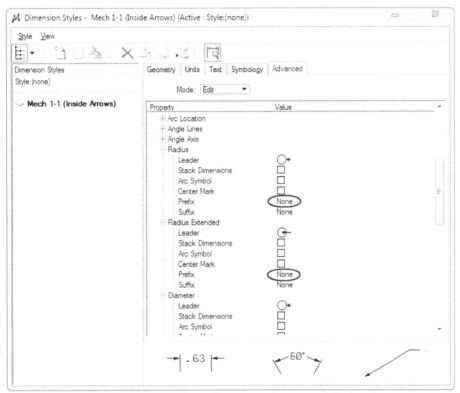

Dimension Style Dialog Box – Advanced Tab Changes

12. You will now need to create one more style. This one will have the arrows to the outside. This works better than having the program deciding when to place the arrows inside or outside.

13. Save the style one more time and then click on the Copy Style tool.

Copy Style Tool

14. Name the style Mech 1-1 (Outside Arrows).

    The only change you will need to make is to set the Text/Terminator settings in the Geometry Tab to Term. Outside.

Text/Terminator Setting Changed for New Style

15. Now you are ready to dimension the drawing.

16. Open the Dimension toolbox and dock it at the top of the screen. Click on Tools, Dimensions, Open as Toolbox.

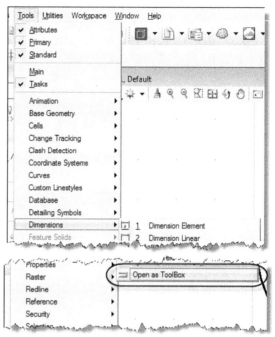

Tools, Dimensions, Open as Toolbox

17. The Dimension toolbox opens. This tool box contains all the tools that you will need to dimension your drawing.

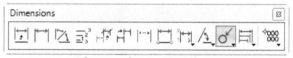

Dimensions Toolbox

18. First you will add the center marks at the two circles.

    Click and hold on the Radial Dimensions: Dimension Radial tool.

    A flyout palette will appear.

    Select the Dimension Center tool to add the center marks.

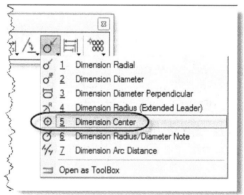

Dimension Center Tool

19. Click on the edge of the arc. You will see a center mark appear. Stretch the endpoints to approximately .25" from the outside edge of the arc.

   Note: The center mark stretches because of the minus sign in front of the value.

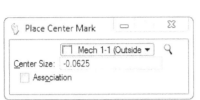

Place Center Mark Tool Settings Box

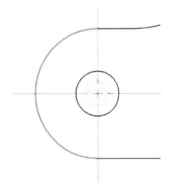

Placing the Center Mark

20. Repeat for the other arc.

21. Click on the Dimension Linear tool to dimension the 6.00 dimension for the two circles.

   Be sure to dimension the circles from their bottom edges and not the centers to preserve the dashes of the center marks.

**Dimensions Toolbox –
Dimension Linear Tool Selected**

   Space the dimension two grid dots or 1/2" from the edge of the object.

6.00 Dimension Placed

22. Add the .50 dimension for the width of the slot.

    Change the style to outside arrows.

    Set the Alignment to True when placing the dimension.

    This way the dimension with be aligned with the feature.

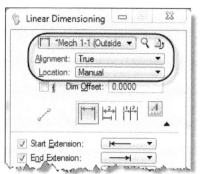

Alignment Set to True

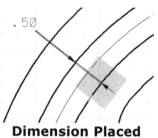

Dimension Placed

23. Switch to the Dimension Radius (Extended Leader) tool. Dimension the arcs as shown.

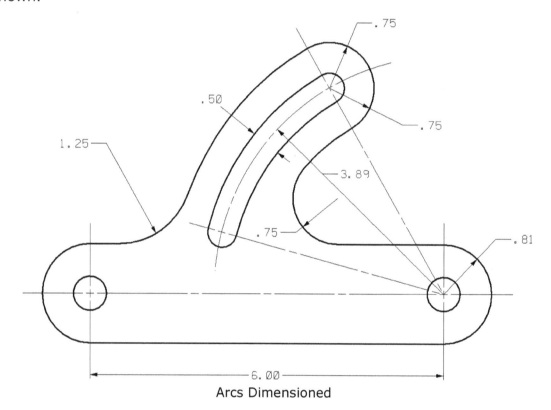

Arcs Dimensioned

24. Use the Dimension Center tool to add the small center marks. Set the Center Size to .0625 (without the minus "-" sign).

25. Edit the text in the radial dimensions to match the example. Double-click on the text to do this.

26. For the diameter dimension on the left side, use the Diameter Extended option in the Radial Dimensions tool.

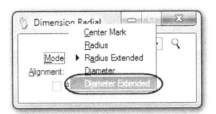

Dimension Extended Option

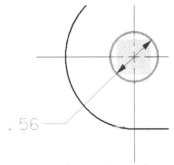

Diameter Dimension Placed

27. Next, dimension the angular dimensions using the Angle Between Lines tool.

   Click on both lines to place the dimension.

   You will need to add a vertical extension line before adding the 30 degree dimension.

Angle Between Lines Tool

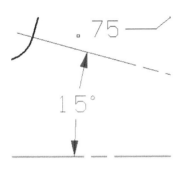

15 Degree Angle Dimension Placed

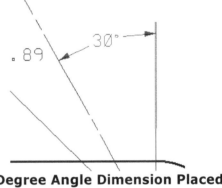

30 Degree Angle Dimension Placed

28. Edit the notes in the upper left corner. Use the edit text command or double-click the text with the element selection tool selected.

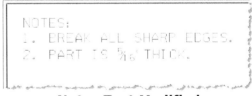

Notes Text Modified

Edit Text Tool

29. Save the drawing.

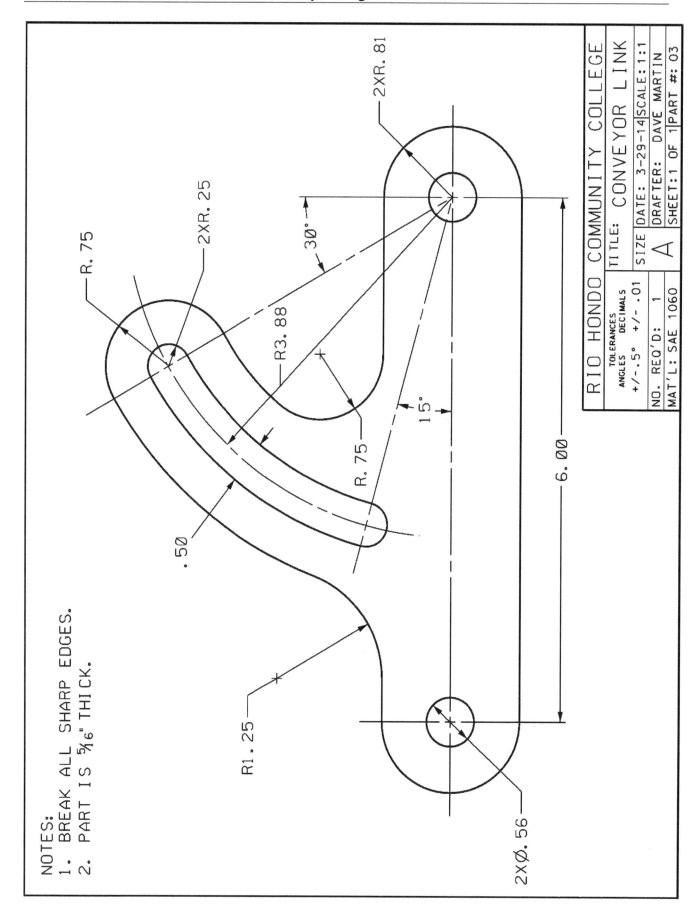

NOTES:
1. BREAK ALL SHARP EDGES.
2. PART IS ⁵⁄₁₆" THICK.

R.75

2XR.25

2XR.81

30°

R3.88

15°

R.75

.50

6.00

R1.25

2XØ.56

RIO HONDO COMMUNITY COLLEGE

TITLE: CONVEYOR LINK

SIZE A

DATE: 3-29-14 SCALE: 1:1

DRAFTER: DAVE MARTIN

SHEET: 1 OF 1 PART #: 03

TOLERANCES
ANGLES   DECIMALS
+/- .5°   +/- .01

NO. REQ'D: 1

MAT'L: SAE 1060

Printing Your Drawing

Description: The procedure will introduce the student to printing their drawings. Two methods will be discussed; printing to a PDF file and to a printer. Creating a Printer Configuration File will also be covered.

Procedure:

In this procedure you will use Project #3 as the example for printing. Printing of the first two projects will also be discussed.

1. Open the Project #3 file and fit the drawing to the view. At this point the drawing should be finished and ready for printing.

2. Click on the Print tool in the Standard toolbox. You may also select the Print tool in the File menu.

Print Tool

3. The Print Dialog box will open.

   Note:
   Your settings will most likely be different than these. Depending of which type of printer is installed, the settings will change.

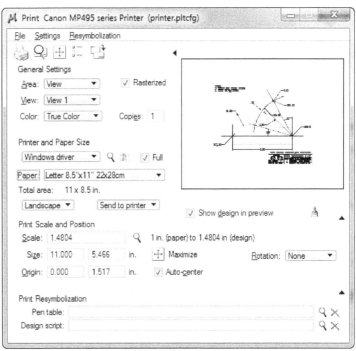
Print Dialog Box

4. At the top left and bottom right corners of the border are small magenta points. These will be the locations for the corners of the fence.

   Note:
   The reason for the points is that if you snap on the border edge it will split the line on the plot and cause the lineweight of the border to appear too thin.

Top Left Snap Point

5. To start the fence around the edge of the border you will need to use a tentative point. You do not need to zoom in to the corner of the border to do this.

    To do this, position the mouse slightly above and to the left of the top left point. Press the right and left mouse buttons at the same time. You will see a tentative point appear.

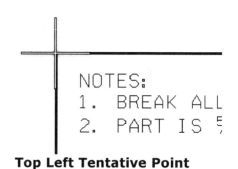

Top Left Tentative Point

6. Click the left mouse to accept and then drag the mouse below and to the right of the lower right snap point.

    The Fence will appear as a green shaded box.

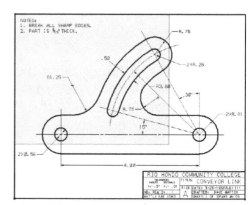

Top Left Fence Corner Placed

7. Repeat the tentative point and click the left mouse button accept the final position of the fence.

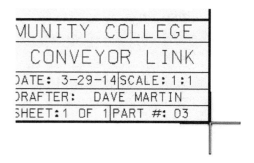

Bottom Right Tentative Point

8. After the Fence is placed, you will see the Area setting in the Print dialog box change to fence. The Drawing view will also file the entire preview window.

    Note:
    Click on the Place Fence tool again to clear the fence.

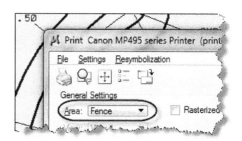

Area Setting Changed to Fence

9. Set the Color Setting to Monochrome.

Color Set To Monochrome

10. Set the Scale Setting to 1.000.

    You will see that the image has resized be slightly smaller than the page size.

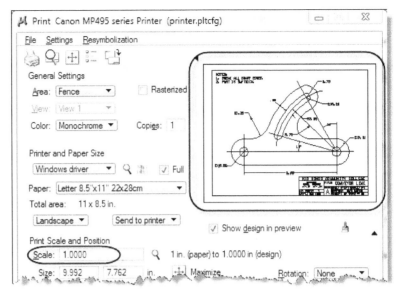

Scale set to 1.000

11. Click the Preview button to preview the print. You may need to enlarge the window to see the lineweight differences.

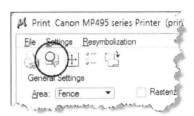

Preview Button

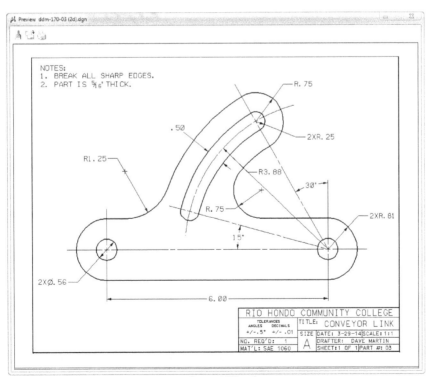

Preview Window

12. Close the Preview window when finished.

13. To send the file to the printer, click the Print button in the dialog box,

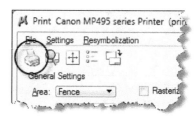

Print Button

14. The drawing will print from the selected printer.

15. To print Projects #1 and #2, use the same settings as before with the exception of the scale.

   Click the Maximize button to size the drawing to the window.

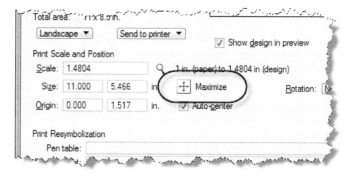

Maximize Button

To Print to a PDF File

- The print settings will be the same to print to PDF file. The change will be to select a different Print Driver.

1. In the Print dialog box, change the driver from Windows driver to Bentley driver.

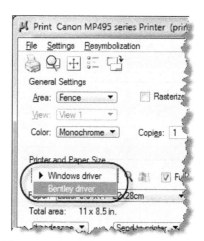

Changing to a Bentley Driver

2. Click the magnifying glass next to the driver pull-down.

Magnifying Glass

3. The Select Print Driver Configuration File box opens.

   Select the pdf.pltcfg file.

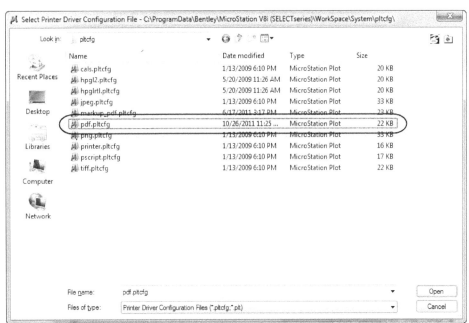

Select Print Driver Configuration File Dialog Box

4. Click Open to select the file and close the dialog box.

5. Reset the scale setting to 1.000 and the Color to Monochrome. The paper size will be ANSI A.

6. Click the Print button in the dialog box. The Save Print As dialog box will open.

7. Set the folder to the location that you wish to save the PDF file.

   Note:
   To avoid having to search for the folder each time, use the Directory History button to display the recent folders used.

Directory History Button

8. Click Save to save the PDF file.

Creating a Print Definition File

- To avoid having to set up a drawing each time you may choose to create a Print Definition File. This file is used to retrieve a file that has been printed and also to save the settings that will be used to print the file. A file must be created for each separate drawing.

1. Click the File Menu in the Print dialog box and choose Save Print Definition File...

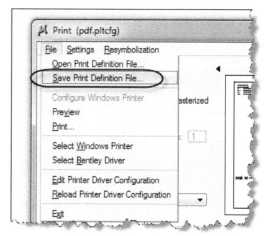

Save Print Definition File

2. The Save Print Definition File dialog box will open.

   Save the file with the same file name as your drawing. The file extension will be .pset.

   Note:
   You may wish to create a sub-folder for the Print Definition files within your drawing folder.

3. Click Save to save the file.

4. To retrieve the file for later use, click on the File menu and select Open Print Definition File... This will open the file and update the saved settings in the Print dialog box.

Project #4

Name: Cover Plate
File Name: Initials-170-04.dgn

Description: The project will introduce the student to the tangent snap mode.

Tools:
- Place Line
- Place Circle
- Construct Circular Fillet
- Attach Reference

- Merge Into Master
- Dimension Linear
- Dimension Radial
- Dimension Diameter

- Edit Text
- Edit Tags
- Fit View
- Partial Delete

Procedure:

The procedure for Project #4 uses similar methods as were used for Project #3. The main thing that the student will be concerned with is the use of the tangent snap mode to create the angled line at the upper left corner of the view.

1. Open Project #3 and save the drawing as Project #4.

2. Attach the Border and Title Block Text files. Merge into Master the text file.

3. Edit the text in the title block and the notes in the upper left corner of the border.

<u>Drawing the Object</u>

1. Draw the R1.50 arc using the Place Arc Tool. Draw the arc with the radius locked and the Start Angle set to 0 degrees. Use the Center, Start method. Sweep the arc approximately 160 degrees in a counter-clockwise direction.

Place Arc Settings

2. Next you will use the Accudraw tool to setup the origin of the R1.88 arc.

    - Click on the Accudraw Coordinate window to activate it.
    - Click once on the Center snap mode in the Snaps Button Bar.
    - Move your mouse to the edge of the R1.50 arc that you just placed.
    - Press the right and left mouse buttons at the same time. You will see a large cross appear at the center of the arc. This is known as a Tentative Point.
    - Click your left mouse to accept the point.
    - When you place the R1.88 arc you will use the Accurdraw Coordinate window to locate it in relation to the center of the other arc.

3. Click on the Place Arc tool.

4. Turn off the Start Angle lock.

5. Click on the Accudraw Coordinate window to activate it. You may also use the F11 key on your keyboard top open/bring focus (activate) it.

6. Move your cursor down and to the left of the origin.

7. Type in the X value at 2 and the Y value at 2.13.

8. Click to begin placing the arc.

9. Click to place the start point of the arc.

10. Drag your mouse and click to place the end point and end the command.

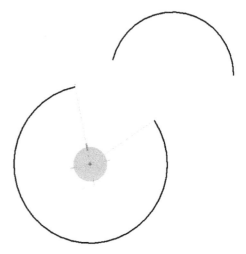

R1.88 Arc Placed

About Accudraw

Using Accudraw effectively requires much practice but can greatly speed up your drafting. There are many shortcuts that you can use.

To open the Accudraw Shortcuts dialog, press the F11 to bring focus to the Accudraw Coordinate window and press the "?" key.

Some shortcuts arte grayed out because they may only be used in a 3D file.

You may want to print this page for reference as you become familiar with the different shortcuts.

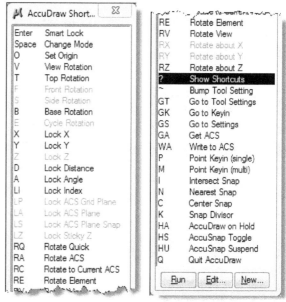

Accudraw Shortcuts

11. Draw the .88 circle by snapping to the center of the larger arc.

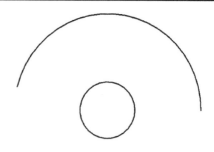

.88 Circle Added

12. Snap a line from the right side of the R1.50 circle down. Come down approx. 1/5 inches.

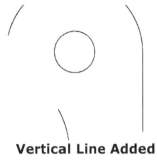

Vertical Line Added

13. Draw a horizontal construction line from the center of the lower R1.88 arc to the right.

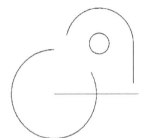

Horizontal Line Added

14. Copy the line with the Move Parallel tool up and down .38 inches.

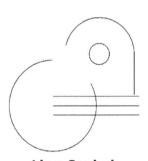

Line Copied

15. Draw a .38 radius arc at the center of the R1.88 arc. Use the endpoints of the line to locate the endpoints of the arc.

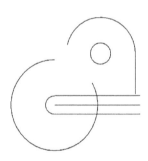

Arc Added

16. Add the R.25 round

    Trim the corner from the vertical line to the top horizontal line

    Delete the horizontal construction line.

Round Added and Line Deleted

17. The last line you will add is the tangent line on the upper left corner of the view.

    You will use the Tangent Snap to do this.

    Double-click on the Tangent Mode in the Snaps Button Bar to activate it.

Tangent Snap Mode

18. Click on the Place Line tool and mouse over one of the arcs. You will see the cursor stick to the arc as you move it.

    Click on the arc. You will see the Solution checkbox appear in the Place Line tool Setting box.

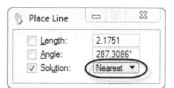

Solution Checkbox

19. Click the mouse to accept the first point. Then mouse over and click the second point.

    Since you double-clicked on the tangent snap mode, it will remain active until you choose another mode.

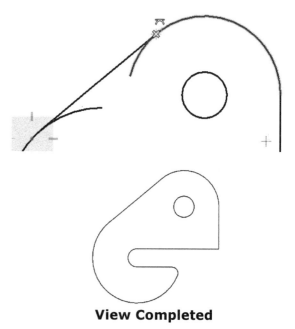

20. Right-Click the mouse to place the line and complete the command.

    Trim the excess line at the tangency.

    The view is finished

View Completed

21. Add center lines and dimensions. You will use the same tools and techniques that were used for Project #3.

22. Save the drawing.

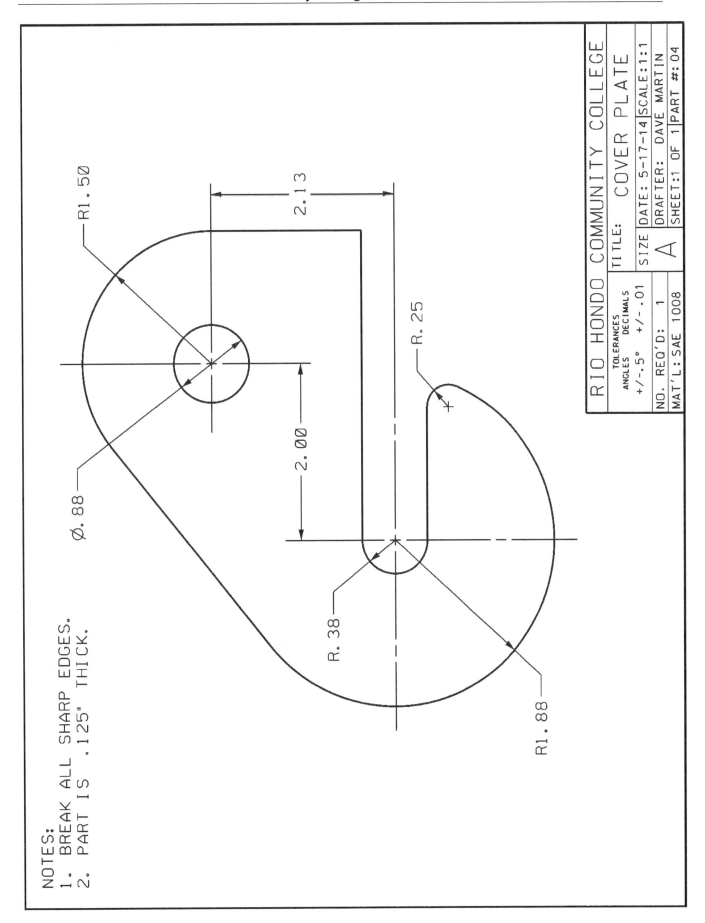

NOTES:
1. BREAK ALL SHARP EDGES.
2. PART IS .125" THICK.

R1.50

Ø.88

2.13

R.25

2.00

R.38

R1.88

RIO HONDO COMMUNITY COLLEGE

TITLE: COVER PLATE

SIZE DATE: 5-17-14 SCALE:1:1

A

DRAFTER: DAVE MARTIN

SHEET:1 OF 1 PART #: 04

TOLERANCES
ANGLES   DECIMALS
+/-.5°   +/-.01

NO. REQ'D: 1

MAT'L: SAE 1008

Project #5

Name: Keyhole Saw Handle
File Name: Initials-170-05.dgn

Description: The project will give the student continued practice using the tangent snap mode.

Tools:
- Place Line
- Place Circle
- Construct Circular Fillet
- Attach Reference

- Merge Into Master
- Dimension Linear
- Dimension Radial
- Dimension Diameter

- Edit Text
- Edit Tags
- Fit View
- Break Element

Procedure:

1. Open Project #3 and save the drawing as Project #4.

2. Attach the Border and Title Block Text files. Merge into Master the text file.

3. Edit the text in the title block and the notes in the upper left corner of the border.

4. Start by drawing the R.88 arc near the middle of the view. You may also draw the view out the border and move them inside before dimensioning.

R.88 Arc Placed

5. Set the origin to the center of the arc using the Accudraw shortcut. Draw the new arc at R2.00 and .31 to the right of the first arc.

    Practice using Accudraw to locate the arc without the aid of construction lines.

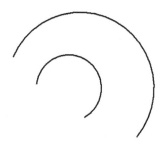

R2.00 Arc Placed

6. Draw a third arc at R.75. The bottom of the arc will be 3.00 to the left at .19 inches down.

    Use the Start, Center method with the following settings...

R.75 Arc Settings

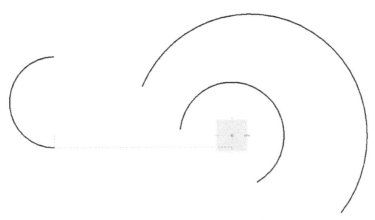

Using Accudraw to Locate the Arc

7. Draw a tangent line from the top of the R.75 arc to the top of the R.20 arc. Trim the excess lines.

    Use the Tangent snap to place the line.

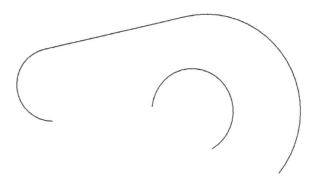

Tangent Line Placed

8. Draw a horizontal line from the bottom of the R.75 arc and a short vertical line from the left side of the R.88 arc.

    The vertical line must be tangent to the arc. You may use the tangent snap and lock the line angle at 270 degrees to do this.

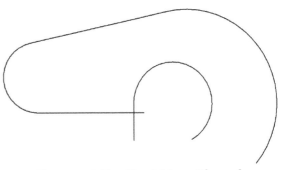

Tangent Vertical Line Placed

9. Fillet the corner using a R.06 arc.

    You should be left with a potion of the short vertical line that connects with the R.06 arc.

**R.06 Arc Placed Using
Construct Circular Fillet Tool**

10. Draw another R.88 arc. The center of this arc will be 1.38 down from the center of the first R.88 arc.

    Use Accudraw to locate the arc center.

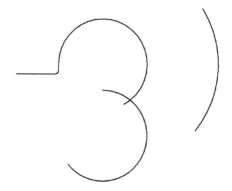

Second R.88 Arc Placed

11. Draw a tangent line vertically from the right side of the R2.00 arc. The line is 1.38 long.

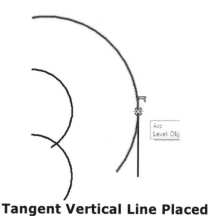

Tangent Vertical Line Placed

12. Draw the next arc using the settings as shown.

    This will locate the arc based off the endpoint of the 1.38 line instead of the center.

    Trim the excess from the R.200 arc.

R.88 Arc Settings

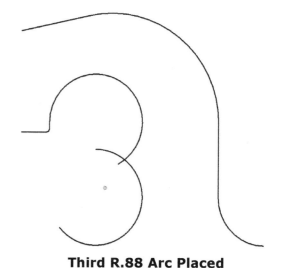

Third R.88 Arc Placed

13. Use the Construct Circular Fillet tool to fillet the two R.88 arcs together.

    The radius is 4.00.

    Pick above and below the centers to the arcs to make sure that the R4.00 arc is facing the right direction.

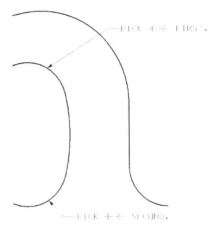

Pick Locations for R4.00 Arc

14. Place the two R2.69 arcs. The center of the left one is at the same center as the top R.88 arc. The second arc center is .88 from the right endpoint of the R 2.00 arc.

First R2.69 Arc   **Second R2.69 Arc**

15. Fillet the two R2.69 arcs together using a R1.00 arc.

Arcs Filleted Together with R1.00 Arc

16. Draw two vertical lines on both sides of the arcs and fillet the corners using a R.06 arc.

    This will also trim the excess off the R.88 and R2.69 arcs.

R.06 Rounds Added

17. The last two features in the front view to locate are the two .25 diameter circles. You will need to draw line from the center of the R.25 arc to the tangency at the top of the R.88 arc.

Tangent Construction Line Added

18. Draw a line from the center of the R.75 arc. You will use Accudraw to create a perpendicular line.

    Start the line at the center.

    Press F11 to bring focus to the Accudraw window.

    Type RQ to use the Rotate Quick shortcut.

    Snap on the midpoint of the line you drew to the tangency of the R.88 arc.

    Move the line down. The line will be at 90 degrees from the midpoint snap.

    Click to place the line. (The length is not important, you will be using the top endpoint to locate the two circles.)

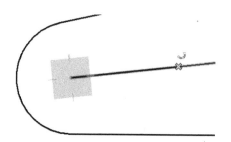

Midpoint Snap to Rotate Accudraw Compass

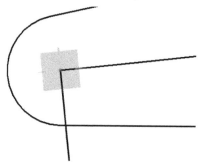

Perpendicular Line Placed

19. Use the Move/Copy Parallel to create three copies.

    The first one is .19 to the right.
    Then another .69.
    Then another .56.

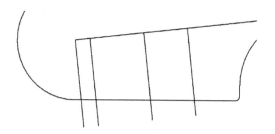

Lines copied

20. Place two .25 diameter circles at the endpoints of the lines.

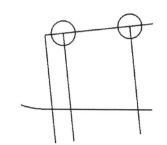

Diameter .25 Circles Placed

21. Extend and trim the next line to the top and bottom of the view.

    Delete the four construction lines.

    Move the last line to the Hidden level.

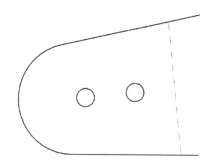

Lines Deleted and Trimmed

22. The front view is completed.

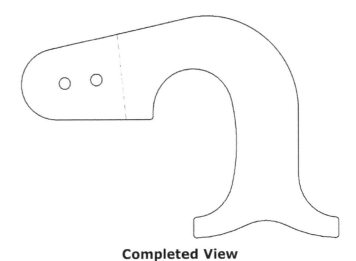

Completed View

23. Draw lines from the features of the front view to the left as shown.

    Use tangent snap and lock the lines at 180 degrees for the lines being projected from the arcs.

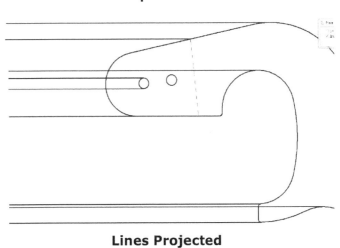

Lines Projected

24. Draw the two vertical lines .75 apart for the right and left sides of the left view.

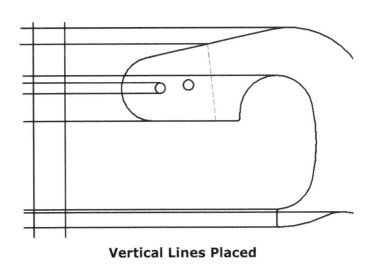

Vertical Lines Placed

25. Use the Move/Copy Parallel command to locate the vertical lines for the .06 wide groove.

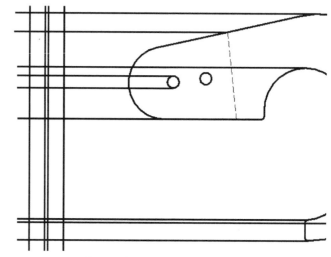

Lines for Groove Placed

26. Use the trim tools to trim the lines to their appropriate intersections.

27. Fillet and round the corners. You will need to change the truncate setting to trim only one of the lines on some of the arcs.

28. Change the appropriate lines to hidden line style.

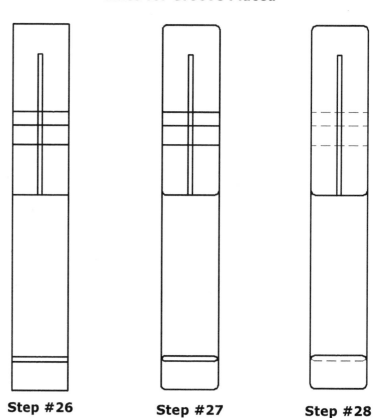

Step #26   **Step #27**   **Step #28**

29. Both views are completed.

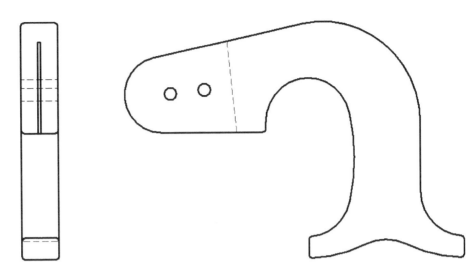

Both Views Completed

30. Use the same techniques and tools to dimension the views.

31. Save the drawing.

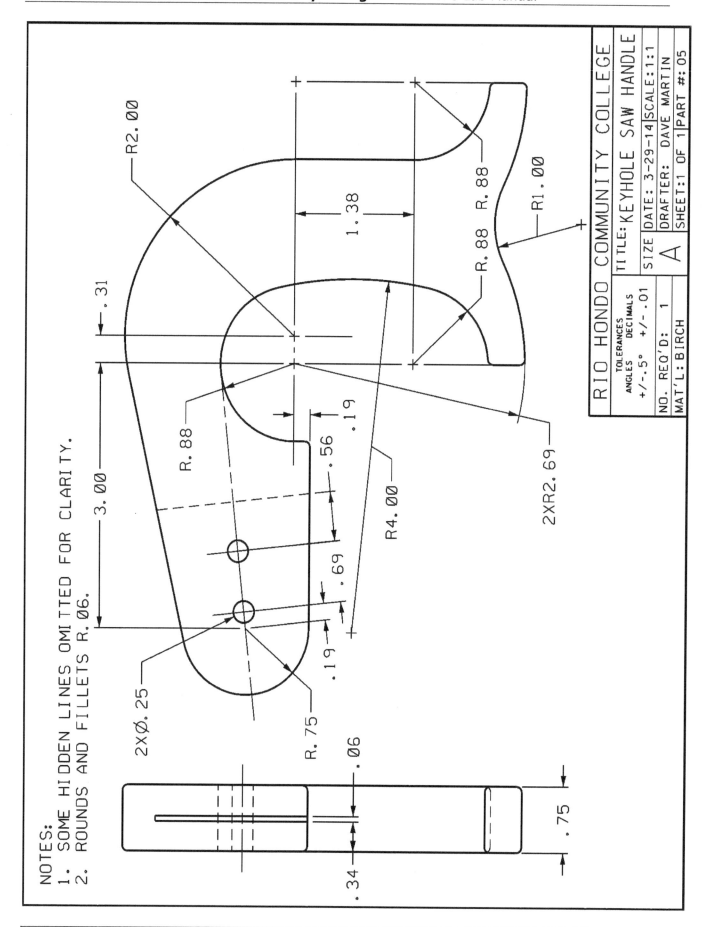

NOTES:
1. SOME HIDDEN LINES OMITTED FOR CLARITY.
2. ROUNDS AND FILLETS R. Ø6.

RIO HONDO COMMUNITY COLLEGE

TITLE: KEYHOLE SAW HANDLE

SIZE A

SCALE: 1:1

DATE: 3-29-14

DRAFTER: DAVE MARTIN

SHEET: 1 OF 1

PART #: 05

TOLERANCES
ANGLES +/-.5°
DECIMALS +/-.01

NO. REQ'D: 1

MAT'L: BIRCH

R2.00
R.88 R.88
R.88
R1.00
2XR2.69
R.88
R4.00
R.75
R.06
2XØ.25

1.38
.31
.19
.56
.69
.19
3.00
.34
.75

Project #6

Name: Hex Bracket
File Name: Initials-170-06.dgn

Tools: • Tools used previously   • Place Regular Polygon   • Mirror

Procedure:

1. After attaching the Title Block and Text files, scale the reference files to 2:1 scale.

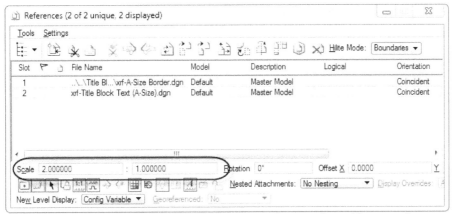

References Dialog Box with Scale Setting Changed

2. Place a 1.00 radius arc.

    Create the 2.00 radius arc and locate 4.00 left from the center of the 1.00 radius arc.

1.00 and 2.00 Radius Arcs Placed

3. Create a tangent line from the top of the 1.00 arc to the top of the 4.00 arc.

Tangent Lines Placed

4. Trim the excess lines as needed and add the 3.00 diameter circle concentric with the 2.00 radius arc.

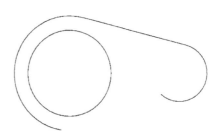

Lines Trimmed and Circle Placed

5.   Mirror the tangent line at the top right portion of the view. Use the center of the 1.00 radius as the mirror point.

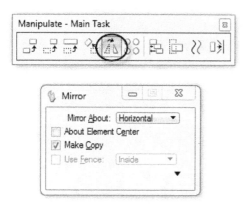

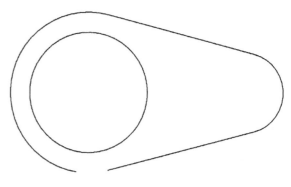

Tangent Line Mirrored

Mirror Tool and Settings

6.   Draw a line at -45 degrees from the center of the 2.00 radius arc. Make the line 3.00 long. Use the Tools settings box to control the length and angle of the line.

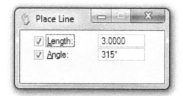

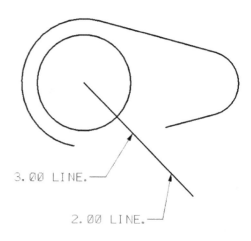

3.00 LINE.⌐

2.00 LINE.⌐

3.00 and 2.00 Construction Lines Placed

7.   Create another line 2.00 long from the endpoint of the first line.

8.   Use the Copy Parallel tool to create a copy of the 2.00 line. Then copy the line inches to the right and left of the line. This will be the edges of the slot.

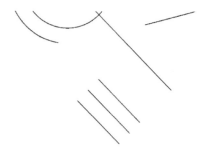

2.00 Line Copied and Edges of Slots Created

9.   Create the two ends of the slot using the Place Arc tool.

     Snap to the endpoints of the lines to place the arcs.

Arcs for Slot Added

10. Delete the original 3.00 and 2.00 construction lines.

    Copy the center line of the slot 1.00 up and to the right.

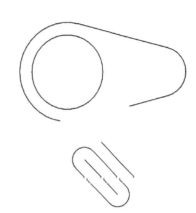

Construction Lines Deleted and Line Copied

11. Delete the center line of the slot and create the R.125 fillet between the mirrored line and the line that was just copied.

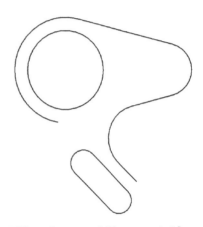

Fillet Arc and Tangent Line

12. Create the hexagon using the settings as shown.

    After placing the hexagon, rotate negative 22.5 degrees.

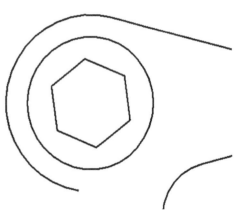

Hexagon Added and Rotated

Polygon Settings

13. Add the 1.00 radius arc concentric with the bottom center of the slot.

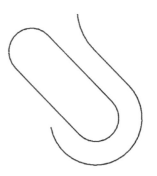

1.00 Radius Arc Added

14. The last object lines you will add for the front view will be the 1.00 diameter circle and the tangent 6.00 radius arc.

    Use the Construct Circular Fillet tool to add the arc.

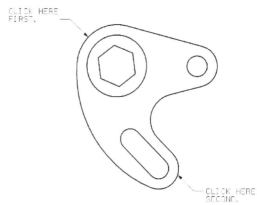

**1.00 Diameter Circle and
6.00 Radius Arc Added**

15. Create the left side view by projecting the edges of the front view.

    Project the tangent edges by switching to the tangent snap mode and locking the line angle at 180 degrees.

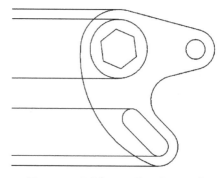

Tangent Lines Projected

16. Project the remaining lines using the Keypoint snap mode.

    After projecting the lines, add vertical lines.

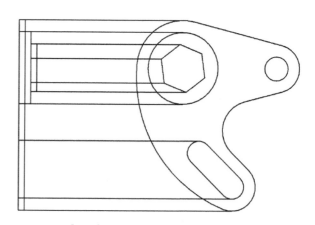

Projecting the Remaining Lines

17. Finish the views by trimming to the appropriate corners.

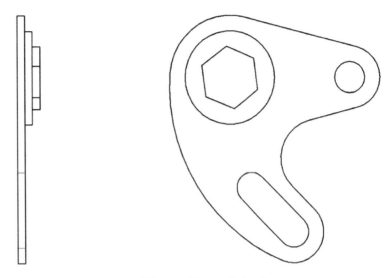

Views Completed

18. Create a two new dimension styles:

    Mech 1-2 (Inside Arrows) and
    Mech 1-2 (Outside Arrows)

    The only settings you will change will be to increase the text size to .25 and the center mark to -0.125 (setting is in the Geometry Tab).

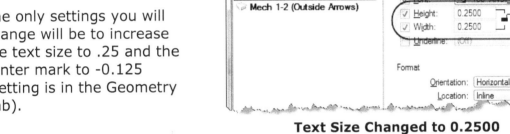

Text Size Changed to 0.2500

Center Mark
    Center Size: -0.1250

Center Mark Size Changed

19. When placing the center lines, the linestyles will need to be scaled up in size to accommodate the 1:2 drawing scale.

    Go to Element Menu, Line Styles, Custom to open the Line Styles Dialog Box.

    Set the scale factor as shown.

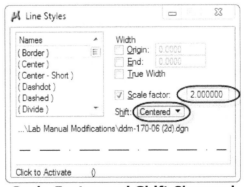

Scale Factor and Shift Changed

20. Place dimensions as shown in the finished example.

21. When placing the Local Note, use the Place Note tool and then add a triangle using the Polygon tool.

    Use an Inscribed polygon and set the radius to .375.

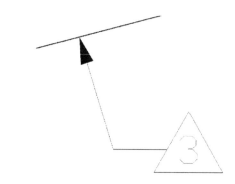

Local Note Placed

22. When dimensioning the locations of the centers of the 1.00 slot, place the 2.00 dimension first and then continue with the 3.00 dimension.

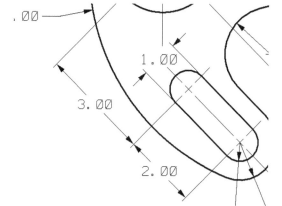

2.00 Dimension then the 3.00 Dimension

23. Save the drawing when finished.

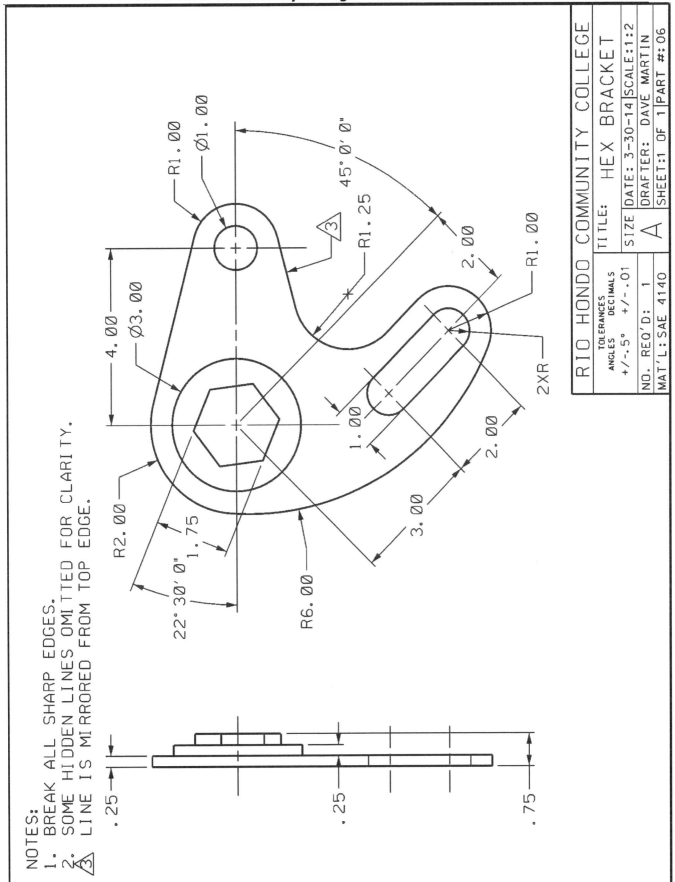

NOTES:
1. BREAK ALL SHARP EDGES.
2. SOME HIDDEN LINES OMITTED FOR CLARITY.
3. LINE IS MIRRORED FROM TOP EDGE.

R1.00
Ø1.00
Ø3.00
4.00
R2.00
22° 30' 0"
1.75
R6.00
R1.25
45° 0' 0"
2.00
R1.00
2XR
1.00
2.00
3.00

.25
.25
.75

RIO HONDO COMMUNITY COLLEGE

TOLERANCES		TITLE: HEX BRACKET	
ANGLES	DECIMALS		
+/-.5°	+/-.01	SIZE	DATE: 3-30-14	SCALE:1:2
NO. REQ'D: 1		A	DRAFTER: DAVE MARTIN
MAT'L:SAE 4140			SHEET:1 OF 1	PART #: 06

Project #7

Name: Gasket
File Name: Initials-170-07.dgn

Tips for completion of the project:

- Scale the Title Block and Text files the same as Project #6.
- Mirror as much of the project as possible. The student will be mirroring along the vertical and horizontal axis.
- Use the Construct Circular Fillet tool to create the rounded corners.

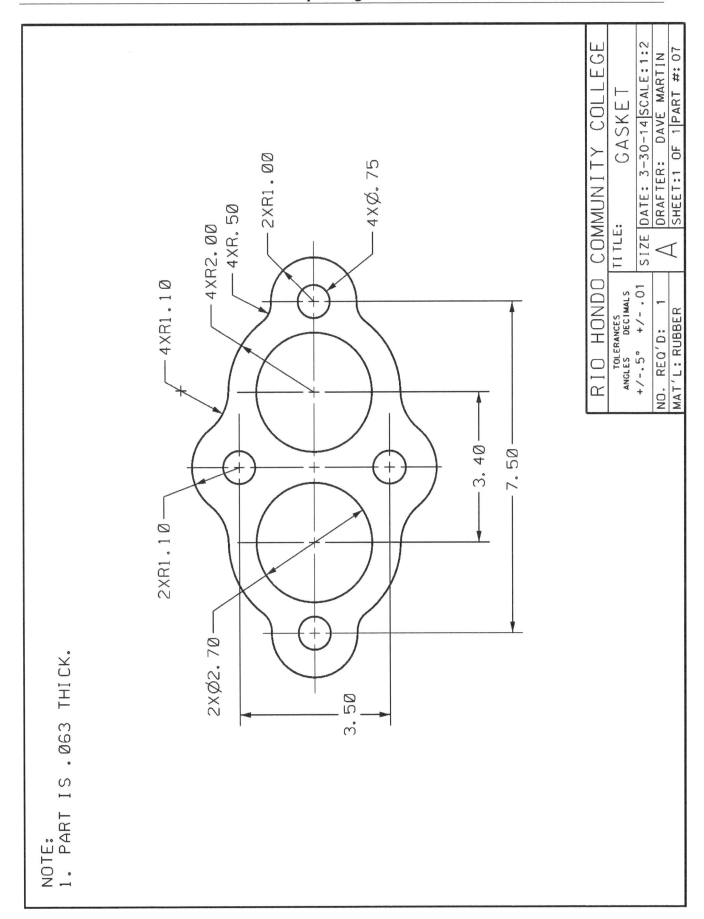

NOTE:
1. PART IS .063 THICK.

4XR1.10

4XR2.00
4XR.50
2XR1.00
4XⱭ.75

2XR1.10

2XⱭ2.70

3.40
7.50

3.50

RIO HONDO COMMUNITY COLLEGE

TITLE: GASKET

TOLERANCES
ANGLES   DECIMALS
+/-.5°   +/-.01

SIZE DATE: 3-30-14 SCALE: 1:2
A   DRAFTER: DAVE MARTIN
      SHEET: 1 OF 1 PART #: 07

NO. REQ'D: 1
MAT'L: RUBBER

Project #8

Name: Adjustable Sector
File Name: Initials-170-08.dgn

Tips for completion of the project:

- This is the first Metric drawing in the manual. Use the appropriate working units before beginning to draw the object.
- Linestyles will need to be scaled up in size to accommodate the metric units.

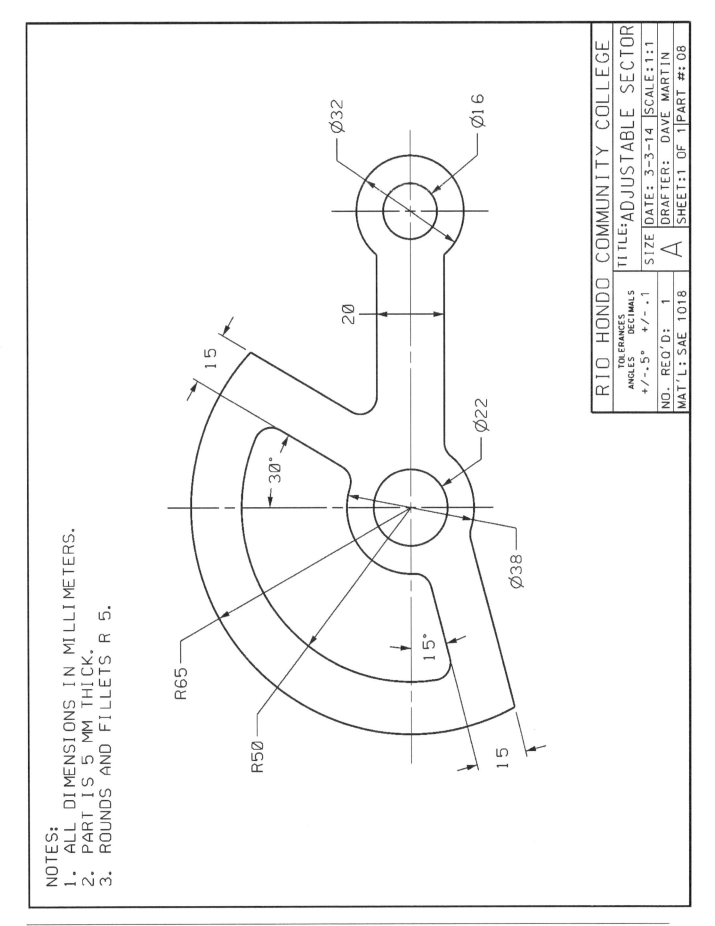

NOTES:
1. ALL DIMENSIONS IN MILLIMETERS.
2. PART IS 5 MM THICK.
3. ROUNDS AND FILLETS R 5.

Ø32

Ø16

20

15

30°

Ø22

R65

R50

15°

Ø38

15

RIO HONDO COMMUNITY COLLEGE

TITLE:ADJUSTABLE SECTOR

TOLERANCES
ANGLES   DECIMALS
+/-.5°   +/- .1

SIZE
A

DATE: 3-3-14

DRAFTER: DAVE MARTIN

SCALE:1:1

SHEET:1 OF 1

NO. REQ'D: 1

MAT'L: SAE 1018

PART #: 08

Project #9

Name: Anchor Plate
File Name: Initials-170-09.dgn

Tips for completion of the project:

- Use the same working units as Project #8. The grids will need to be changed due to the scale of the drawing being 1:2.
- Linestyles will need to be scaled up in size to accommodate the metric units and drawing scale.
- Use the Fillet tool for the R65 radii.

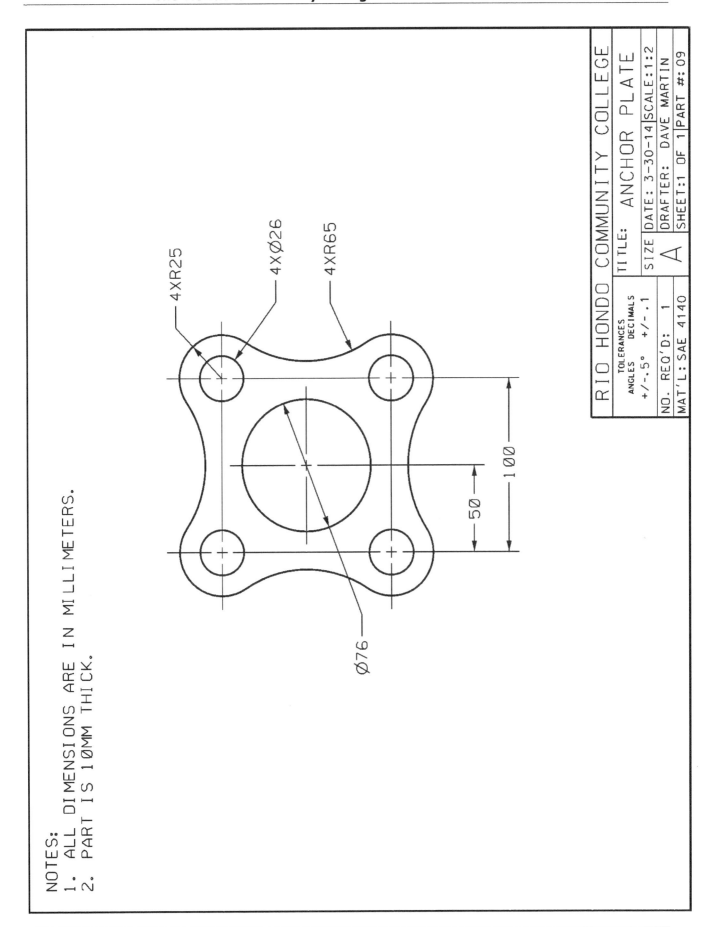

NOTES:
1. ALL DIMENSIONS ARE IN MILLIMETERS.
2. PART IS 10MM THICK.

4XR25

4XØ26

4XR65

Ø76

100

50

RIO HONDO COMMUNITY COLLEGE

TITLE: ANCHOR PLATE

SIZE DATE: 3-30-14 SCALE:1:2

A DRAFTER: DAVE MARTIN

SHEET:1 OF 1 PART #: 09

TOLERANCES
ANGLES   DECIMALS
+/-.5°   +/-.1

NO. REQ'D: 1

MAT'L: SAE 4140

Project #10

Name: Gear
File Name: Initials-170-10.dgn

Tips for completion of the project:

- Linestyles will need to be scaled in size to accommodate the drawing scale.
- Use the Array tool for the holes and the gear teeth.
- Use the Patterning tool for the crosshatching.

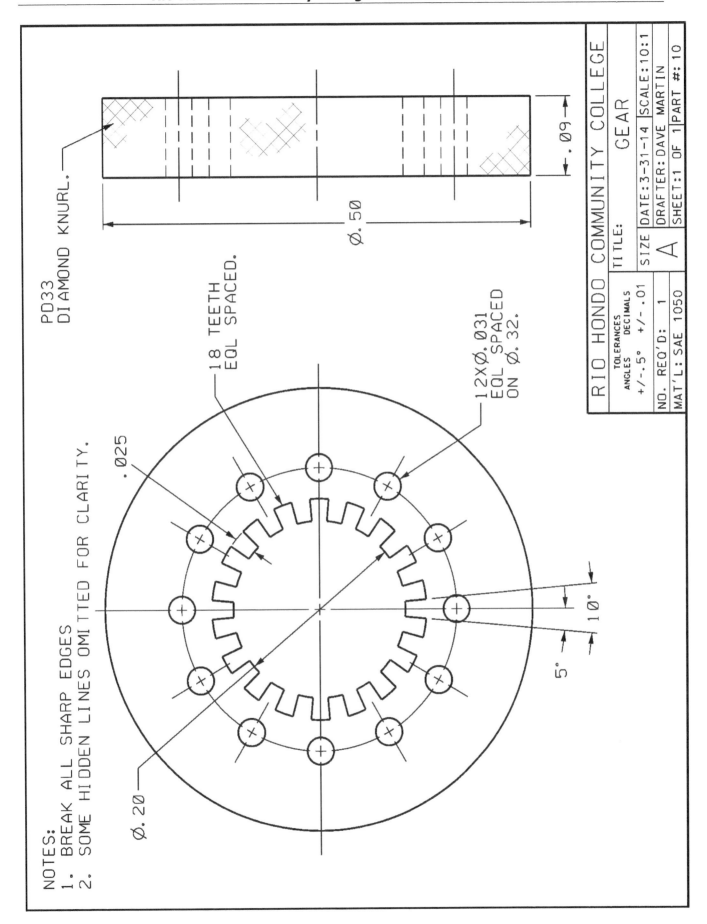

NOTES:
1. BREAK ALL SHARP EDGES
2. SOME HIDDEN LINES OMITTED FOR CLARITY.

PD33
DIAMOND KNURL.

18 TEETH
EQL SPACED.

12X∅.031
EQL SPACED
ON ∅.32.

∅.025

∅.20

∅.50

∅.09

5°

10°

RIO HONDO COMMUNITY COLLEGE

TITLE:

GEAR

TOLERANCES
ANGLES   DECIMALS
+/-.5°   +/-.01

NO. REQ'D: 1

MAT'L: SAE 1050

SIZE

A

DATE: 3-31-14

DRAFTER: DAVE MARTIN

SHEET: 1 OF 1

SCALE: 10:1

PART #: 10

Project #11

Name: Transmission Gasket
File Name: Initials-170-11.dgn

Tips for completion of the project:

- Mirror the top half to the bottom.
- Use the **Partial Delete** tool for the center lines or shift the center line dashes using the **Modify Line Style Attributes** in the **Change Attributes** toolbox.

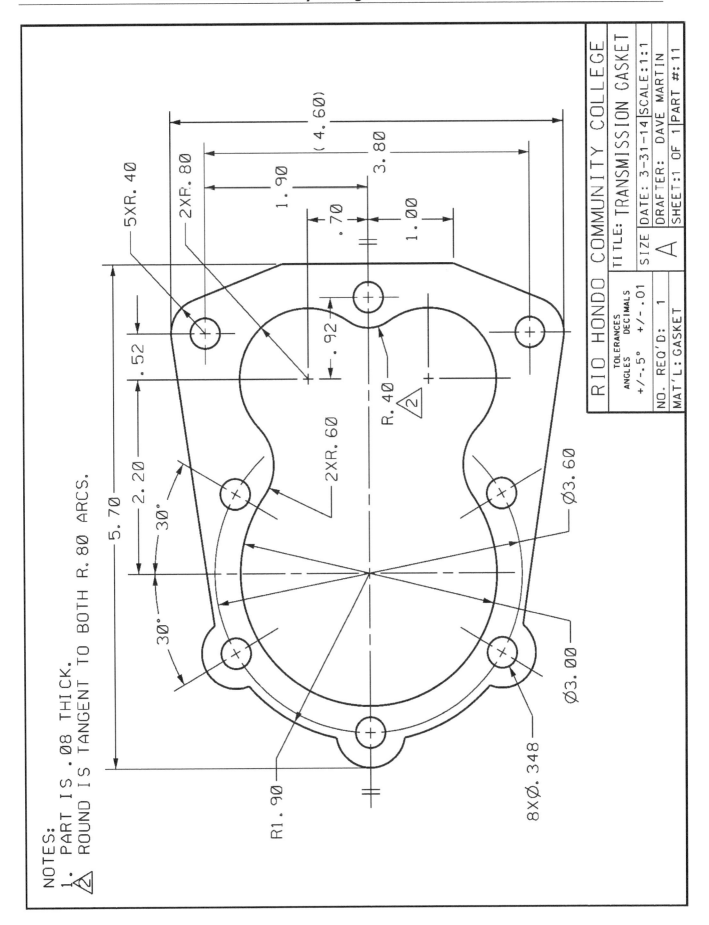

Project #12

Name: Door Closing Arm
File Name: Initials-170-12.dgn

Tips for completion of the project:

- Reference the **B-Size Border file** into the drawing for use as the border.
- Use the settings for a full-scale Metric drawing.
- Create the cross-section using the **Hatch Area** tool.
- Draw the breaks lines randomly with the Line tool. Turn off Accudraw temporarily.
- The Isometric View will be created from the 3D version of the project.

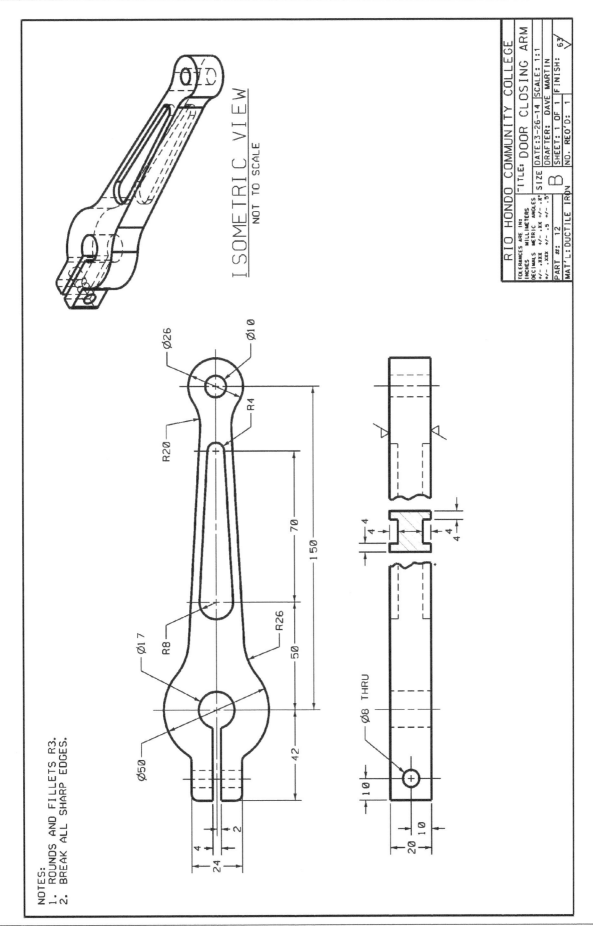

ISOMETRIC VIEW
NOT TO SCALE

NOTES:
1. ROUNDS AND FILLETS R3.
2. BREAK ALL SHARP EDGES.

RIO HONDO COMMUNITY COLLEGE

TITLE: DOOR CLOSING ARM

TOLERANCES ARE IN:
INCHES   MILLIMETERS
DECIMALS   METRIC ANGLES
+/-.XXX +/-.XX +/-.X°
+/-.XXX +/-.5   +/-.5

SIZE DATE:3-26-14 SCALE: 1:1
B   DRAFTER: DAVE MARTIN
      SHEET: 1 OF 1 FINISH:
PART #: 12   NO. REQ'D: 1
MAT'L:DUCTILE IRON

Ø26
Ø10
R4
R20
R8
Ø17
R26
Ø50
70
150
50
42
4
2
24

4
4
4

Ø8 THRU
10
20
10

Caster Assembly Project

This is the explanation for the Caster Assembly Project. The student will complete the parts for the assembly in separate files and then use the 3D Models to create 2D drawings of the parts. 3D and 2D assembly drawings will also be created.

Part/Drawing Description	File Name
3D Model Files	
3D Model of the Post	Initials-170-Caster-01-3D
3D Model of the Bracket	Initials-170-Caster-02-3D
3D Model of the Shaft	Initials-170-Caster-03-3D
3D Model of the Wheel	Initials-170-Caster-04-3D
3D Model of the Bushing	Initials-170-Caster-05-3D
3D Model of the Retaining Ring*	Initials-170-Caster-06-3D
3D Model of the Caster Assembly	Initials-170-Caster-Assm-3D
2D Drawing Files	
2D Drawing of Caster Assembly	Initials-170-Caster-01-2D
2D Drawings of Bracket and Post	Initials-170-Caster-02-2D
2D Drawings of Wheel, Shaft, and Bushing	Initials-170-Caster-03-2D

*Part shape will be referenced from other file.

Workflow:

1. Draw each of the parts of the Caster Assembly in separate files.
2. Create an assembly file for the 3D Assembly drawing.
3. Reference each part into the assembly file.
4. Create two separate Model Views of the assembly; one for the assembled parts and one for the exploded assembly.
5. Create a 2D Exploded Assembly drawing from the 3D assembly model file.
6. Create the 2D drawing for the Post and Bracket by referencing in the standard views from the 3D Model.
7. Create the 2D drawing for the Shaft, Wheel, and Bushing by referencing in the standard views from the 3D Model.
8. Copy the 3D files to the Y: Drive for grading.
9. Print and turn-in the 2D files for grading.

Project Volumes for the Caster Assembly Parts

1. Use these volumes as a guide when turning in the 3D version of your caster parts.
2. The tolerance is the amount that your volume can differ from the volume shown. The +/- means that the volume can be above or below the amount shown by the given value.
3. Use the Measure Volume tool in the Measure palette to measure the volume of your project.

Part Number	Part Name	Volume	Units	Limits of Volume	
				Upper	Lower
1	Post	6435.9452	Cubic Millimeters	6436.0752	6435.8152
2	Bracket	12254.601	Cubic Millimeters	12254.851	12254.351
3	Shaft	2053.3565	Cubic Millimeters	2053.3965	2053.3165
4	Wheel	196217.1304	Cubic Millimeters	196221.1304	196214.1304
5	Bushing	2902.8316	Cubic Millimeters	2902.8916	2902.7716
6	Retaining Ring	89.5737	Cubic Millimeters	89.5757	89.5717

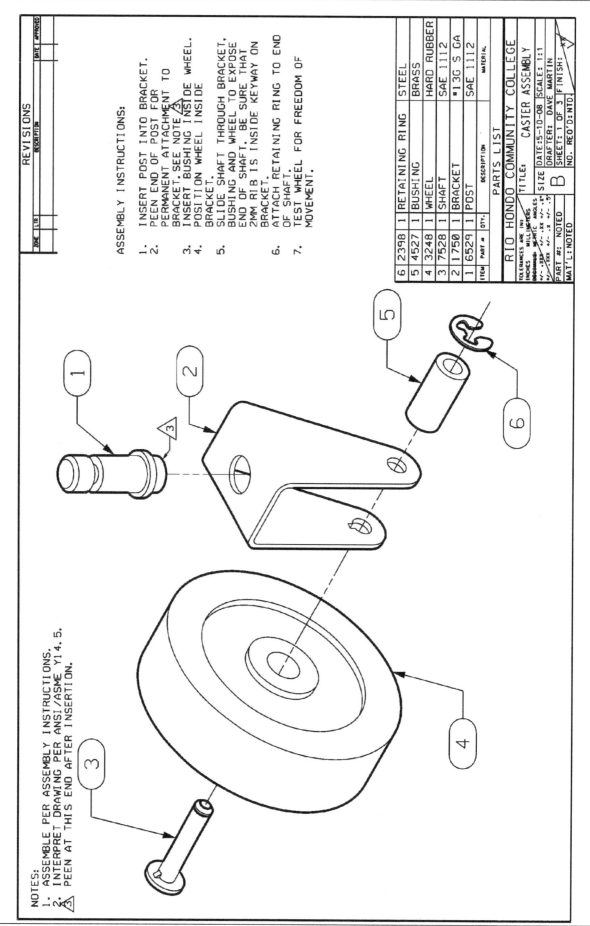

REVISIONS

ZONE	LTR	DESCRIPTION	DATE	APPROVED

ASSEMBLY INSTRUCTIONS:

1. INSERT POST INTO BRACKET.
2. PEEN END OF POST FOR PERMANENT ATTACHMENT TO BRACKET. SEE NOTE 3.
3. INSERT BUSHING INSIDE WHEEL.
4. POSITION WHEEL INSIDE BRACKET.
5. SLIDE SHAFT THROUGH BRACKET, BUSHING AND WHEEL TO EXPOSE END OF SHAFT. BE SURE THAT 2MM RIB IS INSIDE KEYWAY ON BRACKET.
6. ATTACH RETAINING RING TO END OF SHAFT.
7. TEST WHEEL FOR FREEDOM OF MOVEMENT.

PARTS LIST

ITEM	PART #	QTY.	DESCRIPTION	MATERIAL
6	2398	1	RETAINING RING	STEEL
5	4527	1	BUSHING	BRASS
4	3248	1	WHEEL	HARD RUBBER
3	7528	1	SHAFT	SAE 1112
2	1750	1	BRACKET	#13G S GA
1	6529	1	POST	SAE 1112

RIO HONDO COMMUNITY COLLEGE

TITLE: CASTER ASSEMBLY

TOLERANCES ARE IN:	
INCHES MILLIMETERS	
DECIMALS METRIC ANGLES	
+/- .XXX +/- .XX +/- .1°	
+/- .XX +/- .X +/- .5°	

SIZE **B**

DATE: 5-10-08 SCALE: 1:1
DRAFTER: DAVE MARTIN
SHEET: 1 OF 3 FINISH:
NO. REQ'D: NTD.

PART #: NOTED
MAT'L: NOTED

NOTES:
1. ASSEMBLE PER ASSEMBLY INSTRUCTIONS.
2. INTERPRET DRAWING PER ANSI/ASME Y14.5.
3. PEEN AT THIS END AFTER INSERTION.

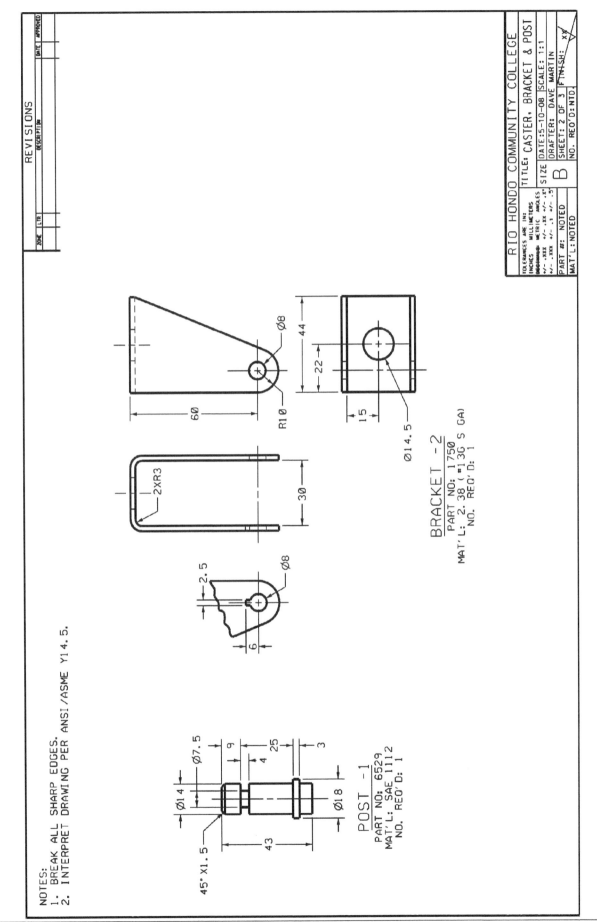

NOTES:
1. BREAK ALL SHARP EDGES.
2. INTERPRET DRAWING PER ANSI/ASME Y14.5.

BRACKET -2
PART NO: 1750
MAT'L: 2.38 (#13G S GA)
NO. REQ'D: 1

POST -1
PART NO: 6529
MAT'L: SAE 11112
NO. REQ'D: 1

REVISIONS

ZONE | LTR | DESCRIPTION | DATE | APPROVED

RIO HONDO COMMUNITY COLLEGE

TITLE: CASTER, BRACKET & POST

SIZE B | DATE: 5-10-08 | SCALE: 1:1
DRAFTER: DAVE MARTIN
SHEET: 2 OF 3 | FINISH: xy

TOLERANCES ARE IN:
INCHES   MILLIMETERS
+/-.XXX   METRIC ANGLES
+/-.XX +/-.X°
+/-.XXX +/-.1 +/-.5°

PART #: NOTED
MAT'L: NOTED
NO. REQ'D: NTD.

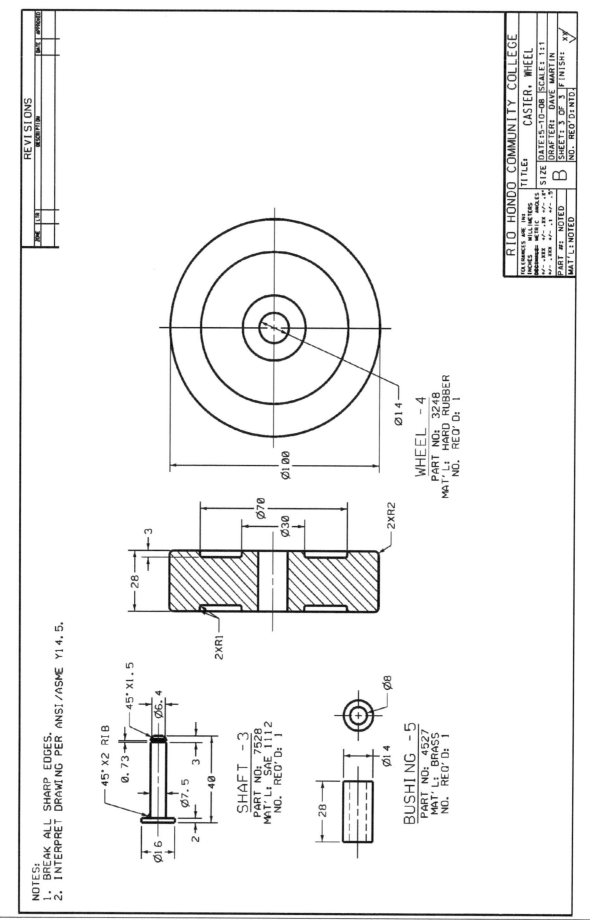

Final Mechanical Project

This is the final mechanical project. This project or the architectural project may be completed. This will introduce the student to the 3d portion of the software. The software will be used to generate the 2d views from the solids.

Name: Robotic Gripper Assembly

File Names: See Below

Part Name	File Name
Gripper Finger	Initials-Gripper-1
Slide Block	Initials-Gripper-2
Pivot Block	Initials-Gripper-3
Cam Follower	Initials-Gripper-4
Shoulder Bolt	Initials-Gripper-5
Air Cylinder	Initials-Gripper-6
.250-28 Nut	Initials-Gripper-7
*Assorted Parts (Cam Follower, Shoulder Bolt, Air Cylinder)	Initials-Gripper-8
*Assembly (Exploded Assembly, Parts List, Assembly Instructions)	Initials-Gripper-Assm

*Parts will be referenced from other files. Only 2D information (Views, Title Block, Dimensions, and Notes) will be added.

Tips for completion of the project:

- Use the Mechanical "B" Size Border file for the template file.
- Using the attached drawings, draw 3d solids of each of the parts.
- Once completed with the solids, reference each part in the sheet view to create the 2d views. Use the B-Size Border files on the network for the 2d drawings.
- Use current practice for the dimensioning.
- Use the mechanical dimensioning style used on the previous drawings.
- The profile of the Air Cylinder is available on the network drive (Y:).

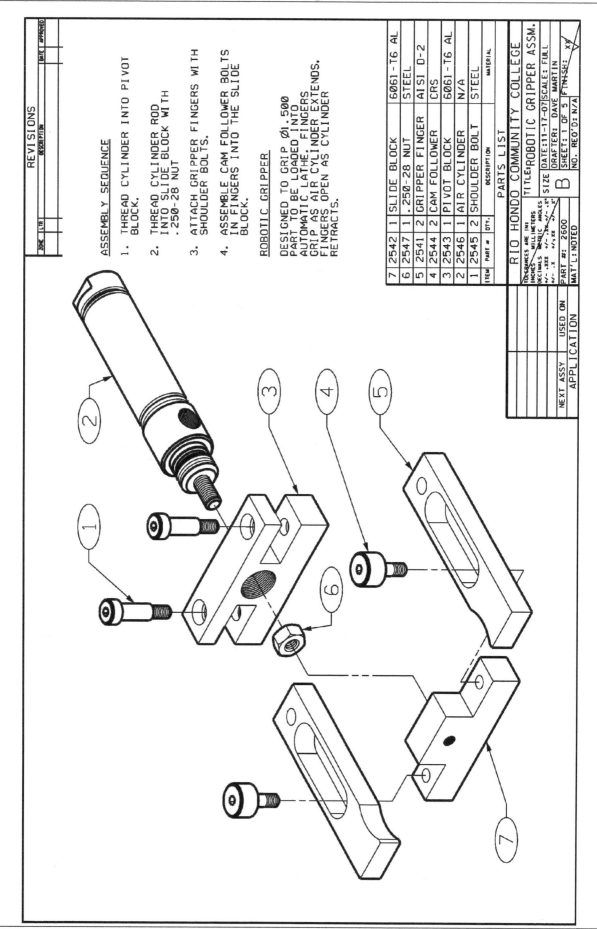

ASSEMBLY SEQUENCE

1. THREAD CYLINDER INTO PIVOT BLOCK.

2. THREAD CYLINDER ROD INTO SLIDE BLOCK WITH .250-28 NUT

3. ATTACH GRIPPER FINGERS WITH SHOULDER BOLTS.

4. ASSEMBLE CAM FOLLOWER BOLTS IN FINGERS INTO THE SLIDE BLOCK.

ROBOTIC GRIPPER

DESIGNED TO GRIP Ø1.500 PART TO BE LOADED INTO AUTOMATIC LATHE. FINGERS GRIP AS AIR CYLINDER EXTENDS, FINGERS OPEN AS CYLINDER RETRACTS.

ITEM	PART #	QTY.	DESCRIPTION	MATERIAL
7	2542	1	SLIDE BLOCK	6061-T6 AL
6	2547	1	.250-28 NUT	STEEL
5	2541	2	GRIPPER FINGER	AISI D-2
4	2544	2	CAM FOLLOWER	CRS
3	2543	1	PIVOT BLOCK	6061-T6 AL
2	2546	1	AIR CYLINDER	N/A
1	2545	2	SHOULDER BOLT	STEEL

PARTS LIST

RIO HONDO COMMUNITY COLLEGE

TITLE: ROBOTIC GRIPPER ASSM.

SIZE B | DATE:11-17-07 | SCALE: FULL

DRAFTER: DAVE MARTIN

SHEET: 1 OF 5 | FINISH: xx

PART #: 2600

MAT'L: NOTED

NO. REQ'D: N/A

REVISIONS

ZONE	LTR	DESCRIPTION	DATE	APPROVED

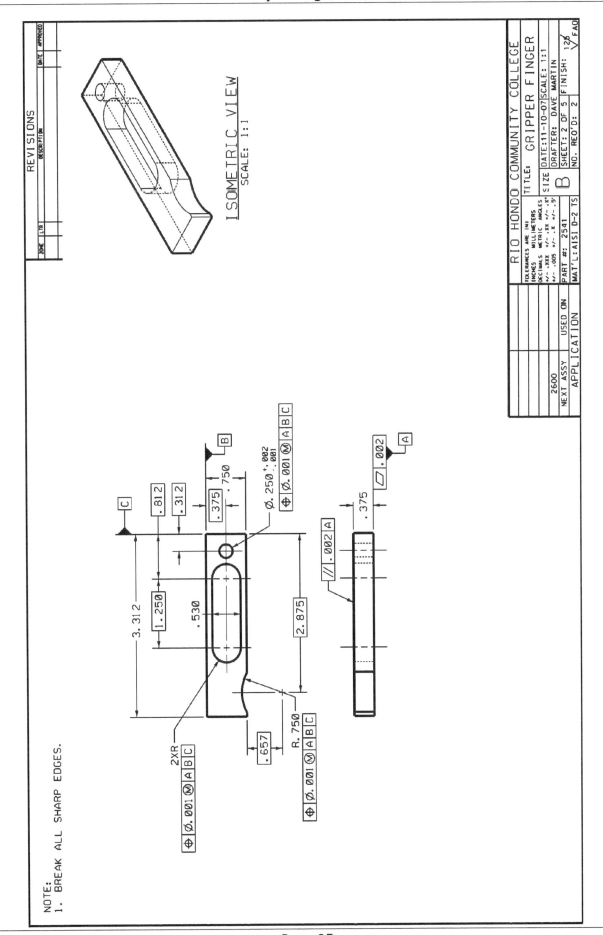

ISOMETRIC VIEW
SCALE: 1:1

REVISIONS

ZONE	LTR	DESCRIPTION	DATE	APPROVED

RIO HONDO COMMUNITY COLLEGE

TITLE: GRIPPER FINGER

SIZE B

DATE: 11-10-07 SCALE: 1:1
DRAFTER: DAVE MARTIN
SHEET: 2 OF 5 FINISH: 125
NO. REQ'D: 2

PART #: 2541
MAT'L: AISI D-2 TS

TOLERANCES ARE IN:
INCHES   MILLIMETERS
DECIMALS METRIC ANGLES
+/- .XX +/- .X°
+/- .XXX +/- .X +/- .5°
+/- .005

NEXT ASSY   USED ON
2600
APPLICATION

NOTE:
1. BREAK ALL SHARP EDGES.

Ø.250 +.002 / -.001

⊕ | Ø.001 Ⓜ | A | B | C

⊘ | .002 | A

// | .002 | A

∠7 | .002

.812
.312
.375
.750
.375
3.312
1.250
.530
2.875
.657
R.750
2XR

⊕ | Ø.001 Ⓜ | A | B | C

C
B
A

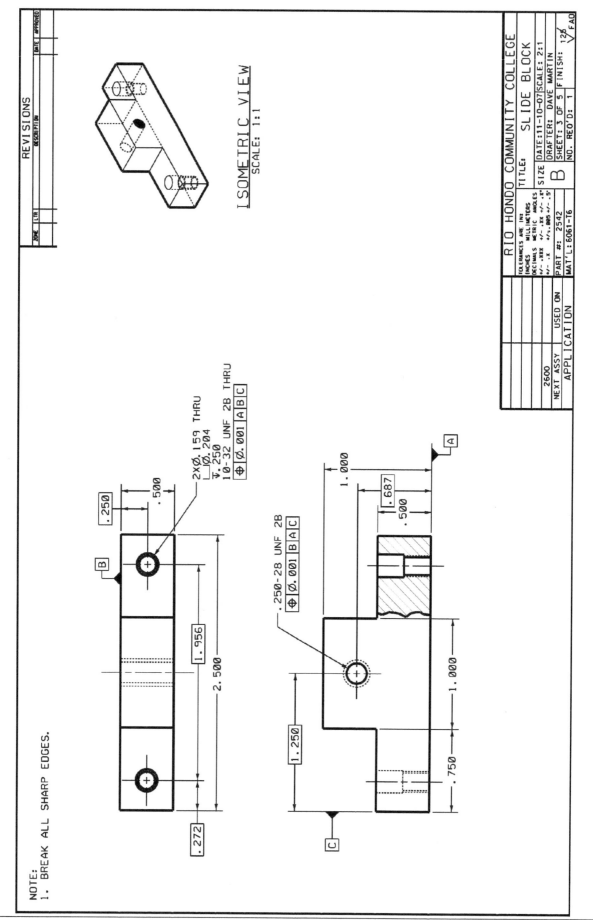

ISOMETRIC VIEW
SCALE: 1:1

REVISIONS

ZONE	LTR	DESCRIPTION	DATE	APPROVED

RIO HONDO COMMUNITY COLLEGE

TITLE: SLIDE BLOCK

TOLERANCES ARE IN:
INCHES   MILLIMETERS
DECIMALS   METRIC ANGLES
+/-.XXX   +/-.XX +/-.X°
+/-.X   +/-.XX +/-.5°

SIZE B

DATE:11-10-07 SCALE: 2:1
DRAFTER: DAVE MARTIN
SHEET: 3 OF 5   FINISH: 125
PART #: 2542
MAT'L:6061-T6
NO. REQ'D: 1

NEXT ASSY 2600   USED ON

APPLICATION

2x Ø.159 THRU
⌴ Ø.204
▽.250
10-32 UNF 2B THRU
⊕ Ø.001 A B C

.250

.500

B

1.956

2.500

.272

.250-28 UNF 2B
⊕ Ø.001 B A C

A

1.000

.687

.500

1.250

1.000

.750

C

NOTE:
1. BREAK ALL SHARP EDGES.

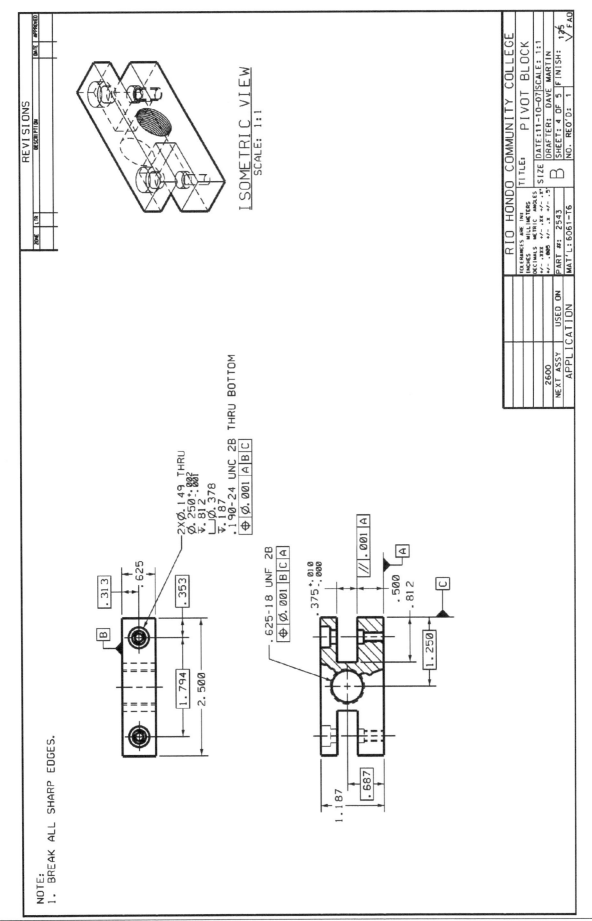

ISOMETRIC VIEW
SCALE: 1:1

NOTE:
1. BREAK ALL SHARP EDGES.

.313

.625

.353

B

1.794

2.500

$2\times\varnothing.149$ THRU
$\varnothing.250^{+.002}_{-.001}$
$\downarrow.812$
$\sqcup\varnothing.378$
$\downarrow.187$
.190-24 UNC 2B THRU BOTTOM
⊕ $\varnothing.001$ A B C

.625-18 UNF 2B
⊕ $\varnothing.001$ B C A

$.375^{+.010}_{-.000}$

// .001 A

.500

A

.812

C

1.250

.001 A

1.187

.687

RIO HONDO COMMUNITY COLLEGE

TOLERANCES ARE IN:		
INCHES	MILLIMETERS	
DECIMALS	METRIC ANGLES	
+/-.XXX	+/-.XX +/-.X°	
+/-.XX	+/-.005	+/-.X +/-.5°

TITLE: PIVOT BLOCK

SIZE B

DATE: 11-10-07 SCALE: 1:1
DRAFTER: DAVE MARTIN
SHEET: 4 OF 5 FINISH: 125
NO. REQ'D: 1

PART #: 2543
MAT'L: 6061-T6

NEXT ASSY 2600
USED ON
APPLICATION

REVISIONS
ZONE LTR DESCRIPTION DATE APPROVED

√ FAO

Page 97

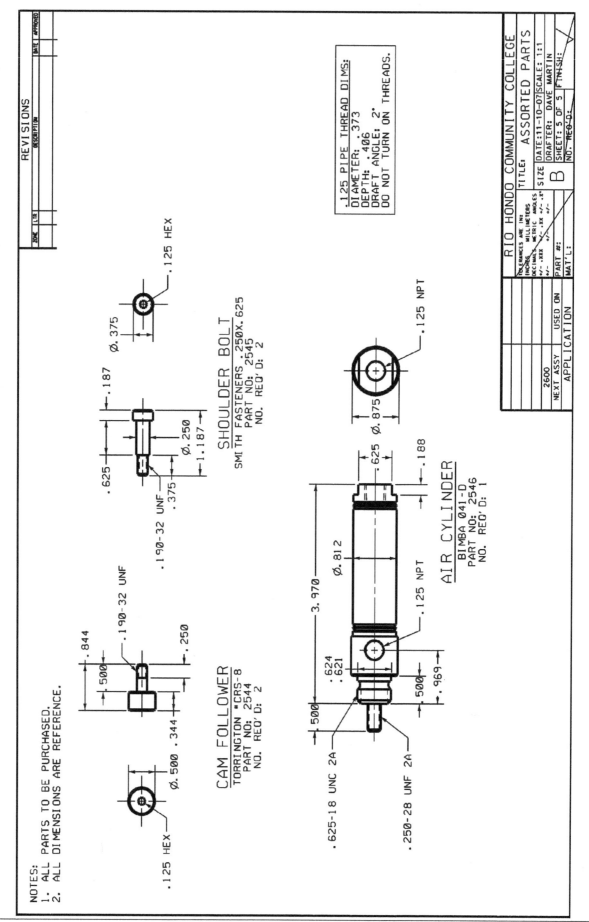

Final Architectural Project

This is the final architectural project. This project or the mechanical project may be completed. This will introduce the student to using the software to complete an architectural project.

The structure that will be drawn is a two-bedroom cabin with a living and dining area. This house also contains one bathroom, which serves both bedrooms.

Name: Two Bedroom Cabin
File Names: See Below

Plotted Files

Sheet #	Drawing Title	File Names	Scale
A-1	Site Plan	Initials - A-1 Site Plan.dgn	1/8" = 1'-0"
A-2	Floor Plan with Door and Window Schedules	Initials - A-2 Floor Plan.dgn	1/4" = 1'-0"
A-3	Foundation Plan	Initials - A-3 Foundation Plan & Detail.dgn	1/4" = 1'-0"
A-4	Exterior Elevations	Initials - A-4 Exterior Elevations.dgn	1/4" = 1'-0"

Other Files

File Name	Description
xrf-Schedule.dgn	Door and Window Schedule to be referenced
xrf-Elevation.dgn	Referenced Elevation Views
xrf-Walls	Referenced Floor Plan with no dimensions
xrf-det-a on a-3.dgn	Referenced Footer Detail

There will also be files created for the plumbing fixtures. These will be available on the Y: Drive.

Tips for completion of the project:

- Use the Architectural "B" Size Border file for the template file.
- Use the Arch.ttf font for the text. See font sheet to create the symbols.

Architectural Font Symbol Key

Arch Font

File Name: Arch.ttf

ABCDEFGHIJKLMNOPQRSTUVWYZ
abcdefghijklmnopqrstuvwxyz
0123456789 ~!@#$%^¢*()

Other Symbols

To use these symbols, hold down the ALT key and type in the 4-digit code on the 10-key pad.

ALT+0176 = ° (Degree Symbol)
ALT+0177 = ± (Plus/Minus)
ALT+0188 = ∡ (Angle)
ALT+0189 = # (Square Feet)
ALT+0190 = ℡ (Floor Line)
ALT+0192 = ℡ (Plate Line)
ALT+0200 = ℄ (Center Line)
ALT+0216 = Φ (Diameter – Large)
ALT+0248 = φ (Diameter – Small)

DOOR & WINDOW SCHEDULE SETUP

USE THE DRAWING BELOW TO SETUP YOUR DOOR & WINDOW SCHEDULE

USE 1/8" SPACING FOR TEXT

SAVE THE DRAWING AS XREF-SCHEDULE.DGN

WHEN COMPLETED, REFERENCE THE DRAWING TO YOUR TITLE BLOCK.

SCALE THE REFERENCE FILE 48.0000 AND ROTATE 90°

DOOR SCHEDULE

SYM	WIDTH	HEIGHT	THK	TYPE	MATERIAL	HC/SC	GLZ AREA	REMARKS
1	3'-0"	6'-8"	1¾"	SLAB	WOOD	SC	–	
2	2'-8"		¾"	SLAB		HC	–	
3	6'-0"			SLIDING			–	
4	6'-0"			SLIDING	METAL	–	40#	¼" TEMPERED GLASS

WINDOW SCHEDULE

SYM	WIDTH	HEIGHT	TYPE	FRAME	SCREEN	GLZ AREA	VENT AREA	REMARKS
A	4'-0"	4'-0"	SLIDING	METAL	YES	16.0#	8.0#	
B	2'-6"	1'-6"			YES	3.8#	.9#	
C	4'-0"	3'-2"			YES	12.7#	6.3#	

¼" TEXT

1/8" TEXT (TYP.)

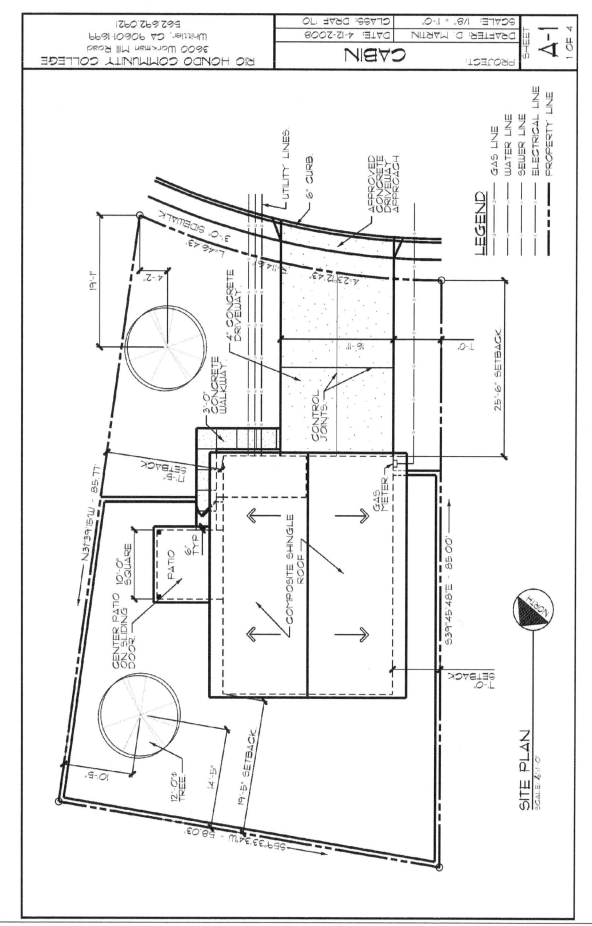

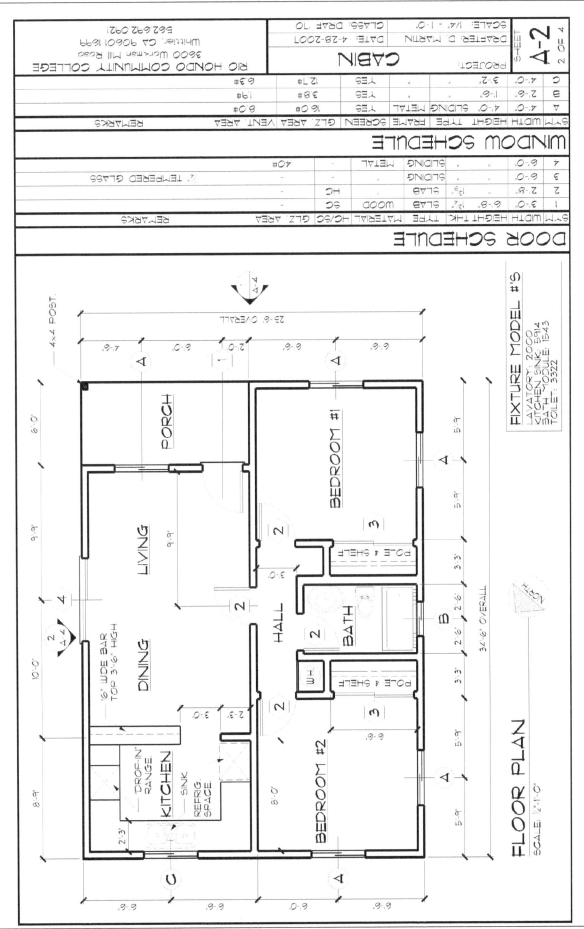

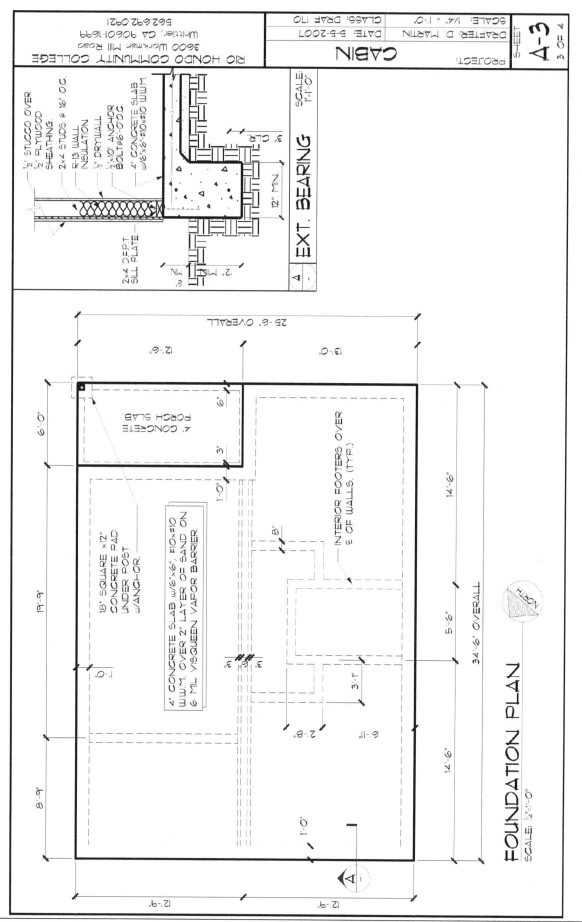

PROJECT:

CABIN

DRAFTER: D. MARTIN	DATE: 5-5-2001	SHEET
SCALE: 1/4" = 1'-0"	CLASS: DRAF 170	**A-3**

3 OF 4

RIO HONDO COMMUNITY COLLEGE
3600 Workman Mill Road
Whittier, CA 90601-1699
562.692.0921

EXT. BEARING
SCALE: 1"=1'-0"

½" STUCCO OVER
½" PLYWOOD SHEATHING
2x4 STUDS @ 16" O.C.
R-13 WALL INSULATION
½" DRYWALL
½"x10" ANCHOR BOLT@6'-0"O.C.
4" CONCRETE SLAB w/6"x6" #10x#10 W.W.M.

2x4 DFPT SILL PLATE

12" MIN.
3"
12" MIN.
3"

FOUNDATION PLAN
SCALE: ¼"=1'-0"

NORTH

25'-6" OVERALL
12'-6"
13'-0"
6'-0"
6"

4" CONCRETE PORCH SLAB.

3"

INTERIOR FOOTERS OVER ℄ OF WALLS. (TYP.)

1'-0"

18" SQUARE x12" CONCRETE PAD UNDER POST w/ANCHOR.

4" CONCRETE SLAB w/6"x6", #10x#10 W.W.M. OVER 2" LAYER OF SAND ON 6 MIL VISQUEEN VAPOR BARRIER

8"
14'-6"
5'-6"
34'-6" OVERALL

19'-9"
1'-0"
3"
3"
3"
3"-1"

2'-8"
6'-11"
14'-6"

8'-9"

1'-0"

A

12'-9"
12'-9"

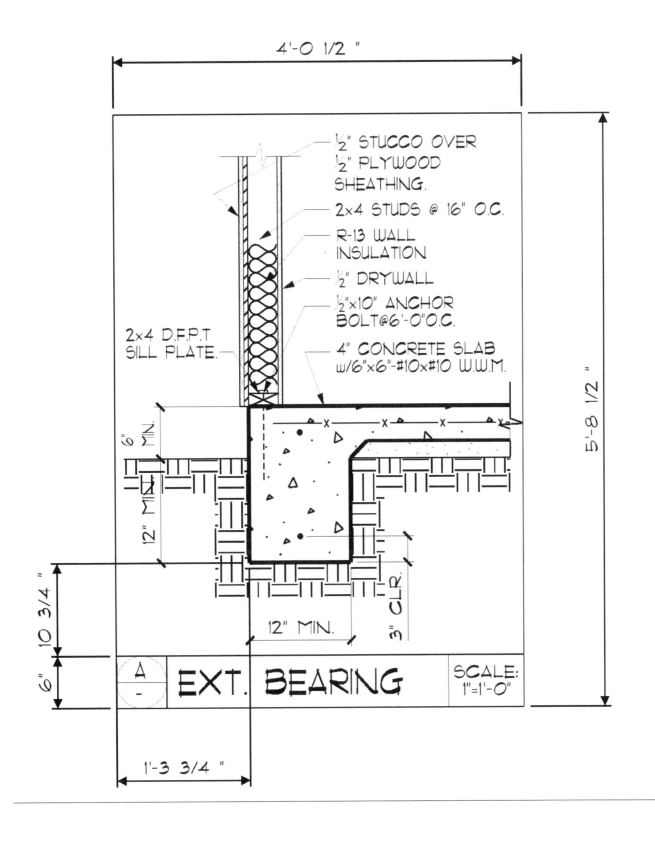

4'-0 1/2 "

½" STUCCO OVER
½" PLYWOOD
SHEATHING.

2x4 STUDS @ 16" O.C.

R-13 WALL
INSULATION

½" DRYWALL

½"x10" ANCHOR
BOLT@6'-0"O.C.

4" CONCRETE SLAB
w/6"x6"-#10x#10 W.W.M.

2x4 D.F.P.T
SILL PLATE.

6" MIN.

12" MIN.

10 3/4 "

6"

12" MIN.

3" CLR.

5'-8 1/2 "

A
-
EXT. BEARING

SCALE:
1"=1'-0"

1'-3 3/4 "

RIO HONDO COMMUNITY COLLEGE

DRAFTING 170 MicroStation for Basic CADD Applications

Portfolio of Architectural & Mechanical Projects

INSTRUCTOR: DAVE MARTIN

NAME: YOUR NAME HERE

DATE: DATE SUBMITTED

SEMESTER & YEAR SUBMITTED

RIO HONDO COMMUNITY COLLEGE

DRAFTING 170 MicroStation for Basic CADD Applications

Portfolio of Mechanical Projects

INSTRUCTOR: DAVE MARTIN

NAME: YOUR NAME HERE

DATE: DATE SUBMITTED

SEMESTER & YEAR SUBMITTED

Conclusion

Congratulations on completing the class! You now should have a basic understanding of the MicroStation V8i software. This software is used in the Architectural, Civil, Geospatial, and Plant Management. With these skills you possess a valuable commodity.

If you wish to learn more of the 3d side of the software, it is recommended that you take the ENGT 280 and/or the ARCH 280 classes. These classes teach more of the three - dimensional capabilities of the software. The AECOsim software is covered in the ARCH 280 class.

There are many jobs available that require knowledge of the MicroStation software. Many municipalities such as Los Angeles Department of Water and Power (DWP) use this software for the design and maintenance of public utilities. This software is also used for the design of government buildings and sites for the General Services Administration.

Once Again, Congratulations!

Sincerely,

Dave Martin
Rio Hondo Community College
Instructor
January, 2015

www.ingramcontent.com/pod-product-compliance
Lightning Source LLC
LaVergne TN
LVHW060145070326
832902LV00018B/2959